Archaeology of Psychotherapy in Korea

This is the first book in English dedicated solely to the historical development of psychotherapy in Korea. It is an archaeological research of literature relating to the care and treatment of mind in Korean history in dialogue with spiritual, philosophical, cultural, social, and medical perspectives. It reviews the evolution of different approaches on mental illnesses covering autochthonous practices, psychiatry, clinical psychology, counselling, Western psychotherapy, and Korean psychotherapy. *Archaeology of Psychotherapy in Korea* inspects:

- Folk treatment
- First psychiatry
- Influence from clinical psychology
- Counselling development
- Implementation of Western psychotherapy
- Shaping of Korean psychotherapy.

Its discussion engages firmly with the Korean culture and perspective while acknowledging various extrinsic influences and the fact that Korean psychotherapy continues to evolve in its own unique manner. It aims to refine the understanding of psychotherapy development in Korea in connection with its historical and social backgrounds, and to interpret a way to highlight the culturally relevant psychotherapy that is more suitable as a Korean psychotherapy better attuned to the distinct cultural and societal expectation of Korea.

Haeyoung Jeong is a psychotherapist and art therapist. She received her doctorate in Psychotherapy Sciences from the Sigmund Freud University, Vienna.

Routledge Studies in Asian Behavioural Sciences
Series Editor: Lo Tit Wing, City University of Hong Kong

Archaeology of Psychotherapy in Korea
A study of Korean therapeutic work and professional growth
Haeyoung Jeong

Archaeology of Psychotherapy in Korea

A study of Korean therapeutic work and professional growth

Haeyoung Jeong

Routledge
Taylor & Francis Group
LONDON AND NEW YORK

First published 2015 by Routledge

2 Park Square, Milton Park, Abingdon, Oxfordshire OX14 4RN
711 Third Avenue, New York, NY 10017

Routledge is an imprint of the Taylor & Francis Group, an informa business

First issued in paperback 2018

British Library Cataloguing in Publication Data
A catalogue record for this book is available from the British Library

Library of Congress Cataloging in Publication Data
Jeong, Haeyoung, author.
Archaeology of psychotherapy in Korea: a study of Korean therapeutic work & professional growth / by Haeyoung Jeong.
p. ; cm.
I. Title.
[DNLM: 1. Mental Disorders—therapy—Korea. 2. Psychotherapy—history—Korea. 3. History, 20th Century—Korea. 4. History, 21st Century—Korea. WM 11 JK6]
RC480.5
616.89'1409519—dc23
2014021399

ISBN: 978-1-138-79380-4 (hbk)
ISBN: 978-1-138-58022-0 (pbk)

Typeset in Times
by Book Now Ltd, London

Dedicated to the people on the Sewol ferry and to families and friends affected by the incident

Contents

Illustrations

Foreword

This book by Haeyoung Jeong is a remarkable one as it is presumably the first book about psychotherapy in Korea which describes both 'worlds': the Western worldview of psychotherapy and the Korean view on psychotherapy, both from an historic perspective.

For me as a Western-trained psychoanalytic psychotherapist, it is very informative to discover what a rich tradition has existed in Korea since ancient times about the nature of the human soul and its treatment. With the spreading of Western psychotherapy all over the world and also in Korea, the author turns to national history, seeking its roots and looking for the integration of the past with the future and the West with the East.

The author is in good company with Sigmund Freud who described psychoanalysis as a method of 'archaeology of the soul'. Haeyoung Jeong is the archaeologist and psychoanalyst of the understanding of the collective soul, its theories and practices of Korea.

She does not deal with political circumstances but has chosen a more spiritual and philosophical way of looking beyond everyday life to excavate the real trunk of understanding the soul in Korea from former times to now. She stays in a line of Henri Ellenberger's book on the *Discovery of the Unconscious* (1970) but also of Michel Foucault's efforts to look behind the curtain of normal conventions and she looks for the drives and forces which constitute modern consciousness in the mirror of its history.

With this book, the global understanding of the soul makes a step forward and it enriches the scientific but also the cultural understanding of Korea and its capacities, as well as its problems. This is also shown through the illustrations of the book which gives me one more dimension of the topic.

Dr Alfred Pritz
President of the Sigmund Freud University
Vienna, May 2014

Ship-Jangsaeng 십장생

To enjoy a long healthy life in harmony with nature is a prime ideal throughout Korean culture. It is the main goal of Korea's indigenous *Shin-shun* (Spirit-Immortal) Ideology that permeates and colours its Shamanism, Buddhism, Confucianism, other traditions and folk-culture. One motif from this tradition that is still most commonly used and considered meaningful is the *Ship-Jangsaeng* 십장생 that is the Ten Symbols of Longevity: Rock, Tortoise, Sun, Crane, Deer, Mountains, Reishi mushroom, Water, Pine trees and Cloud. These are the ten items that represent immortality.

Chronology of events

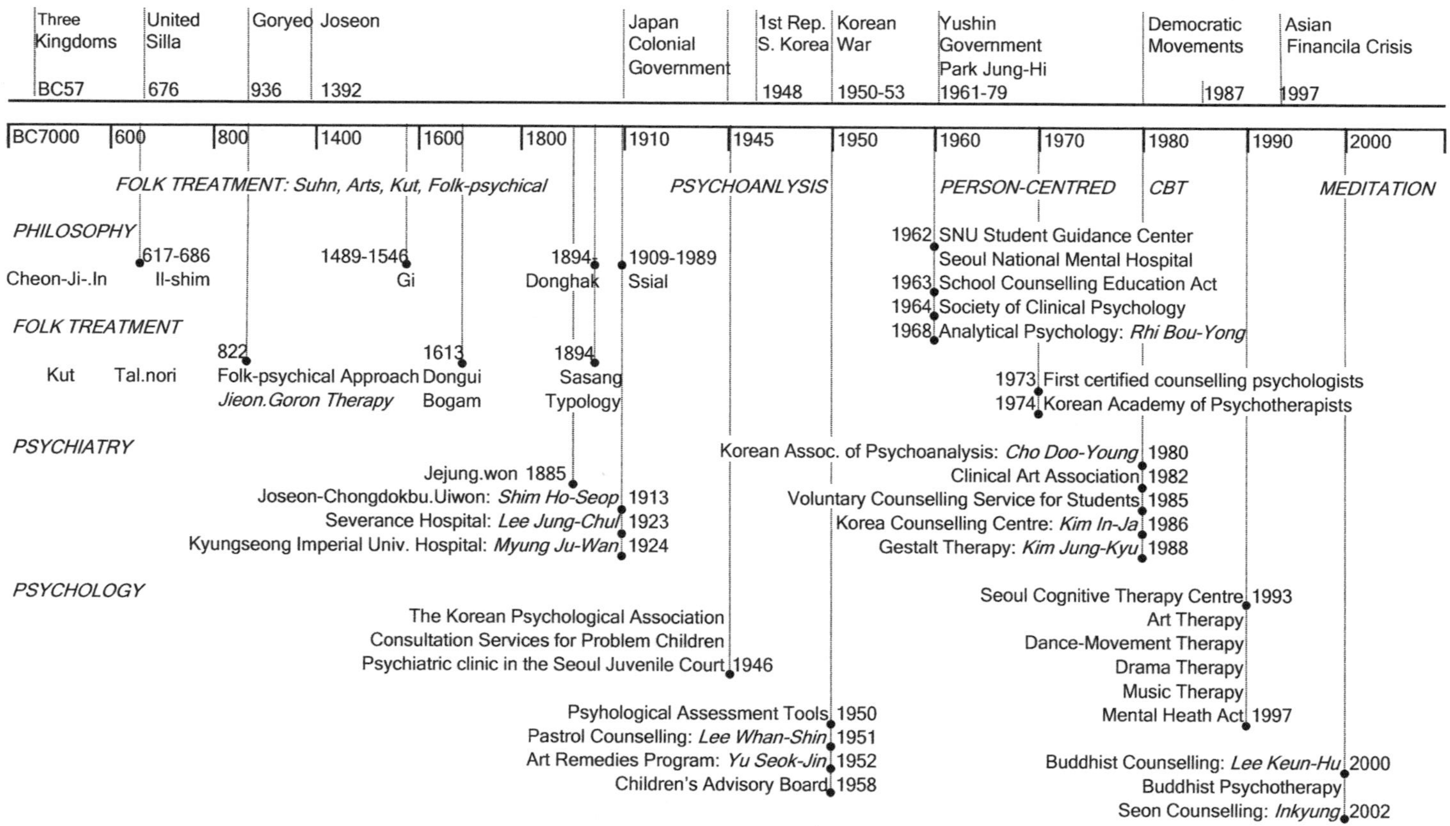

Introduction

Historically, in Korea, mental illness and its treatment were largely a matter for spiritual healers, such as shamans, Buddhist monks and Taoist priests, and even Confucian scholars. In fact, shamanistic healing, Buddhist and *Tao* philosophy and practice of meditation, the Confucian cultivation of mind, together with folk-psychical methods of traditional Korean medicine have all been preserved throughout Korea's history. The first documented record of individual psychotherapy in Korean history may be the case of treating the 'depressed' Chungkong in 822. A Confucian scholar named Nokjin who recognised the nature of his illness effected the cure by 'proper words and high discourse', a method also mentioned in traditional Eastern medicine, that is similar to modern didactic psychotherapy.

In the 1930s, the theories of modern Western psychotherapy were introduced into Korea, and some Korean psychiatrists attempted to apply the concepts of Freudian psychoanalysis or methods of hypnosis and persuasion in their treatment. However, due to the extreme discrimination against Koreans' access to training and profession by the colonial Japanese government, their activities were limited; before liberation in 1945, psychotherapy in Korea barely existed. During the Korean War, the Koreans came in contact with American dynamic psychiatry, psychological tests, clinical psychology and the Western modes of counselling. From the 1950s, many mental health professionals emerged from various disciplines, allowing psychotherapy in Korea to grow and evolve.

In the last two decades, while Western psychotherapy has continued to develop and swell the number and types of therapy, the psychotherapy in Korea has also suffered from an internal struggle. Professional psychotherapists who have been trained in Western modes of therapy have commonly faced difficulties because of the particular nature of Korean patients' expectations, relation formation and responsiveness. Questioning the default application of Western modes of psychotherapy without validating their suitability in the Korean setting, a number of dedicated mental health professionals have promoted the integration of traditional Korean values and practices with the Western methods of psychotherapy. The main effort taken by these professionals has been to combine locally familiar notions of the *Tao* and Buddhist philosophy and methods of meditation. Another related accomplishment comes from the field of expressive arts therapy, incorporating traditional Korean artistic activities such as *tal-nori* (mask play), *samul-nori* (percussion music play) or *madang-nori* (open yard arts play).

To refine the understanding of psychotherapy development in Korea, this book traces the treatment of mental issues throughout its recorded history. It explores traditional Korean thoughts, beliefs and values as the backbone of therapy and reviews the development of different attitudes, approaches and methods for addressing mental illness in relation to their historical and social contexts. The book begins by revealing the important cultural-specific concepts considered vital to understanding Korean ethno-psychology, Korean ways of thinking and feeling. Four core concepts are introduced and they are *Haan* (deep grief or resentment), *Jeong* (strong feeling of affection or attachment), *Noonchi* (intuitive perception) and *Heung* (intrinsic sense of joy). It is followed by the four main streams of religious and ethical experience (i.e., Shamanism, Buddhism, Confucianism and Christianity), which played a definite role in forming the Korean mentality or consciousness. The notions of *Cheon-Ji-In* (the connected 'oneness' of heaven, earth and humans) and *Pungryu* (aspiring toward nature and harmony; a natural lifestyle usually associated with creativity and spontaneity) are also explored. The subsequent text examines the significant practice of arts play as a primordial treatment, followed by the contributions of shamans and shamanic rites and traditional Korean medicine.

These first three chapters really provide the horizontal overview on the Korean mental geography and the practices served to soothe its rifts and fissures. In the following three chapters, the developments of first psychiatry, clinical psychology and counselling are explained focusing on the growth of each professional domain. Outlining the achievement of expressive arts therapy, the Western methods of psychotherapy, classified into the three categories of psychoanalytic, humanistic and cognitive behavioural psychotherapy are then investigated. Finally, the developments of Taopsychotherapy and psychotherapy through Buddhist teaching or practice of meditation are highlighted, and thereby completing the holistic knowledge-base of how present day, Korean psychotherapy has been shaped.

Drawn upon the understanding of psychological, spiritual, ethical, cultural and medical characteristics in the historical development of mental treatment in Korea, this book attempts to highlight the importance of knowledge about its cultural and philosophical history and the historical conditions obscured behind system or custom, in order to appreciate the true nature and challenges of Korean psychotherapy. It takes the view that such knowledge is essential to identify a psychotherapeutic approach that is better attuned to the specific needs of Koreans within their cultural milieu. The book shines from the perspective of a Korean psychotherapist inquiring not 'what is Korean psychotherapy?', but 'how is Korean psychotherapy patterned; how has Korean knowledge of mind cure historically developed and changed?'.

The idea of the archaeology of psychotherapy comes from Foucault's archaeology of knowledge. While the book tracks his methodology of archaeological analysis only loosely, it treads its path by unearthing and distinguishing the strata of ideas that constitute the approaches for mental cure over the past centuries. It reveals layers of diverse practices for the treatment of the mind, and attempts to produce a form of knowledge pertaining to the distinctive character of Korean psychotherapy today and thereby establish the foundations for more suitable and effective practices.

The word 'psychotherapy' has two Korean terms; one is *Simli-Chiryo* 심리 치료 (心理 治療) and the other is *Jungshin-Chiryo* 정신치료 (精神 治療). Both *Simli-Chiryo* and *Jungshin-Chiryo* are Sino-Koreans words.[1] The latter has a more psychiatric connotation of 'mental' treatment and is used amongst psychiatrists. On the other hand, *Simli-Chiryo* originated from the Chinese for psychology (*Simli*, 心理) (心 literally meaning 'mind or heart' and 理 meaning 'logic or reason') and *Chiryo* (治療) meaning treatment. This is more generally used by other mental health professionals. *Naedam-ja* 내담자 is a Sino-Korean word to refer to a counsellee. *Nae* (來) meaning 'to come', *dam* (談) 'to talk' and *Ja* (者) 'a person', *Naedam-ja* thus literally means 'a person who comes to talk'.[2] *Simli-Chiryo* can be then paraphrased as dealing with the logic of mind of a person who comes to talk. This book is about the history, evolution and context of *Simli-Chiryo* 심리치료 in Korea.

Notes

1 Today, in South Korea, the core of the Korean vocabulary is made up of *Hangeul* 한글, the native phonetic alphabet of the Korean language, while a significant proportion of the words especially that denote abstract ideas, are Sino-Korean words called *Hanja* 漢字; *Hangeul* 한글 was created in 1443 but only came into widespread use in the late nineteenth century replacing Chinese characters. *Hanja* is words that originated from Chinese, or were heavily influenced by Chinese words and coined in the Korean language. In North Korea, officially, *Hanja* has not been used since June 1949 and many words borrowed from Chinese have been replaced with native Korean words.

2 The Korean word for counselling is *Sangdam* 상담, a coined Sino-Korean word. *Sang* (相) means 'one another' and *dam* (談) means 'talk'. The character 相 can be split again into 木 (tree) and 目 (eye). 談 can be split into 言 (word) and 炎 (flame). 상담 (相談), then, can be read as 'to talk looking at one another around a fire', exquisitely evoking the idea of 'a calm, gentle, willing and glad dialogue'.

1 Korean mental geography

Korean ethos

Two approaches to the pursuit of Korean psychology are manifest today. One approach deals with Shamanism, Buddhism and Confucianism to find the elements which may be understood and reinterpreted from the viewpoints of modern psychology. Another approach is from folk psychology, espousing social constructivist philosophy.[1] Psychologists in this line derive important cultural-specific concepts from Koreans' spoken words and analyse the relationships of the concepts. Holding on to these Korean terms, they enquire into characteristic phenomena of Korean life and present them as psychological concepts. Notably Choi Sang-Chin 최상진 (1940–2011)[2] has pioneered such research on the psychology of Koreans since the 1980s in the dominant academic milieu of studying it through using the terms and theories of Western psychology. He devoted himself to developing a Korean indigenous psychology and the psychological conceptualisation of many indigenous phenomena. Today, concepts such as *Haan* 한, *Jeong* 정, *Noonchi* 눈치 and *Heung* 흥, that reflect the essence of Korean psychology in both cultural characteristics and interpersonal relations, are culture-specific concepts considered vital to understanding Korean ethno-psychology – Korean ways of thinking and feeling.

Haan 한

Haan is a key word to the understanding of Korean people and culture. It has a very complex cultural, psychological structure and has a highly subtle in-depth psychological dynamic, running on many levels from the highest historical national consciousness extent to the innermost feelings of an individual. Historically, *Haan* has been regarded as a Korean person's historical, cultural, social and collective emotional state of repressed and accumulated anger, resulting from an appalling national history of invasions and wars, as well as from a painful personal life of poverty, exploitation and losses. Its geographical positioning exposed the country to frequent invasion and occupation by neighbouring foreign forces – a repeated experience of being trampled and destroyed. Koreans have experienced an abundance of loss and pain in their lives. In the twentieth century, Korea was occupied by Japan for 35 years (1910–1945) and endured the Korean War that killed millions of people, ending with the tragic division of the Korean Peninsula. Warfare together with deep political upheavals caused Koreans grievous destruction, personal loss, unbearable pain and suffering. In addition, the social injustice of the traditional Confucian system in particular generated its own degree of personal misery and victimisation for the ruled. The poor, the powerless, as well as women, had to be subservient and cope with much maltreatment and injustice. Within this history and culture, few have escaped the experience of loss, suffering or resentment. For their own survival and with the overall inclination to live in harmony, however, they have mostly suppressed their real emotions, thereby fostering deep feelings of *Haan.*

Haan is generally understood as the psychological state that usually appears as one is overcome by the anger arising from suffering injustice or anything that is unfairly inflicted upon an innocent person or a group, for a prolonged period. Not only invading foreign forces, an unequal society or abusive parents-in-laws, but even fate or natural calamity can generate the *Haan* feeling of indignation. While the original Chinese character of *Haan* 恨 means 'to get even with' or 'to revenge', and thus has a more action-oriented vengeful sense, the Korean use of *Haan* 한 (恨) stresses a suppressed feeling of anger. Of this suppressed anger, the grief and agitation for one's appalling condition is repeatedly aroused and subdued in one's mind. When suffering reaches an extreme, one collapses into a compressed feeling of sadness, despair and bitterness. This accumulated feeling of chagrin, resentment and rancour that occurs as a result of prolonged deficiency, mistreatment, unfairness or injustice for a long period of time defines *Haan*.

Choi Sang-Chin described the process of *Haan* in four phases. The first phase is the experiencing of anger, resentment, hatred or desire for vengeance for an injustice or mistreatment. Given the other Korean cultural tendency not to risk social relationships, the pressure is to suppress this anger. Being prohibited from expressing the experienced anger outwardly, from unknotting or acting out the anger, one turns to self-blame, surrendering to fate, nihilism or some rationalisation that could reduce the intensity of the anger. In the second phase, anger turns into sadness, frustrated desire into feelings of helplessness and desire for revenge into self-hatred; depression and pessimism become pervasive. The third phase is the period when one keeps re-thinking and questioning the situation. Feelings of sadness or agitation are aroused and subdued repetitively. A Korean theologian, Ahn Suk-Mo 안석모 (1953–2013) noted that *Haan* of this phase carried the image of 'wounded-ness', the shattered and split self and life almost akin to mourning. This phase may last a long time. It is usually while experiencing this phase of *Haan* that Koreans come to discuss it. In the fourth phase, one begins to detach and objectify the *Haan* feeling by putting emotional distance between *Haan* experiences, and can talk about it more calmly. The melancholic sentimentality of *Haan* of this last stage has been typically expressed in a sublimated way in singing, writing and other art forms.

Korean psychiatrists assert that *Haan* is deeply imprinted in the collective subconscious of the Korean people, and that is a symbol of the Korean psyche and the Korean version of victimisation syndrome. From a psychiatric viewpoint, *Haan* is regarded as a 'causative factor' in the development of a Korean culture-bound syndrome called *Hwabyung*. It literally means 'fire' (*hwa* 화; 火) and 'disease' (*byung* 병; 病) translated as 'anger disease'. *Hwabyung*, known for a long time in Korea as a folk-medical term, is now registered as one of the culture-bound syndromes in the appendix of the Revised *Diagnostic and Statistical Manual of Mental Disorders* (DSM IV), published by the American Psychiatric Association. It notes *Hwabyung* as a folk syndrome specific to Koreans, as an anger syndrome attributed to the prolonged suppression of anger. The related symptoms are fatigue, indigestion, discomfort in the abdomen, anorexia, fear of impending doom, panic, dysphoria, generalised aches and pains, palpitations and insomnia.

Haan-puri 한풀이

While generally understood as a provenance for fulminating anger, *Haan* is also regarded as a motor force for accelerating Korea's remarkable economic success and modernisation, and as a principal source of Koreans' fervour for education. Another outcome often attributed to *Haan* is the strong motivation and will to persevere and fight on until an objective is achieved. *Haan* of poverty and oppression became a drive for Koreans to work hard to excel and be successful. *Haan* of socio-political oppression was sometimes expressed as in violent social revolution and anti-government demonstrations often including chants and dances – ritualistic expressions of their *Haan* and *Haan*-rage.

Haan has also been understood as a source for creation. *Haan* that underlies repressed emotions or unrequited yearnings, thereby inordinate frustration and anger, was often sublimated into arts. *Haan*-related stories derived from their daily life experiences were the most common and popular themes for Korean folklores and literature. Many cultural heritages, including *tal-nori* (mask play), *madang-nori* (open yard arts play), *pan-sori* (epic chant), folk paintings and ceramic arts have been related to people's *Haan* and widely practised to overcome one's *Haan*. Koreans sought to release their *Haan* by means of dance, music, drama and painting. Naturally *Haan* has formed a nucleus of traditional Korean arts and culture. In this respect, the creativity in Korean people is, without doubt, partially ascribed to *Haan* as a major source of energy. Korean Shamanism was another area in which traditionally Koreans sought to deal with their *Haan*. For instance, shamanic rituals called '*Kut* 굿' are thought to release one's *Haan* by resolving the *Haan* of the spirits of the dead. *Kut* is akin to a symbolic drama with plenty of singing and dancing in which people are often invited to join in. It has played an important part in Korean life.

Historically and culturally, Koreans have developed various ways to deal with *Haan*. *Haan* has been transformed, sublimated or fermented into energy for life, for creation, or for the production of socially meaningful results including arts and social reformation. The action and process of unknotting and letting out *Haan* is called *Haan-puri*. It usually denotes 'wish-fulfilment'. Today, these traditional dynamic, expressive and artistic methods of releasing *Haan* are, however, fading away.

Jeong 정

Jeong is another Korean term of cultural-specific affect. The related Chinese character 情 is also used in Japan. However, there is a subtle distinction in its meaning for each country. The Chinese emphasise the aspects of 'loyalty and reciprocity' when using their *Jeong* character, whereas the Japanese equivalent, pronounced '*jyo*', means rather sentimental feelings usually used with another word '*nin* (human)' as '*nin jyo* 人情'. *Jeong* in Korean culture has a much more ambiguous and subtle meaning in its use. It refers to a psychological sense of bonding or relational tie with a person, extending to a place, an object or anything that one has constructed a lasting sentimental relationship with over time. *Jeong* occurs through direct or indirect contact, or mutual experiences and it is aroused autonomously, spontaneously and unconsciously.

Jeong is a central concept in describing the quality of relationship in any dimension. It represents a more primitive way of relating, of being more fused and less separated. The interactions among family members that emphasise oneness, sameness, mutual support and even sacrifice manifest the prototype of *Jeong*-based relationships. It is this *Jeong* that makes Koreans say 'we' rather than 'I', 'our mother, our house' rather than 'my mother, my house'; it links to '*Uri* 우리 (we)' culture of Koreans. Such psychology of 'we-ness' or *Jeong* relationship is frequently extended to relationships with non-family members. Once the 'other' enters a sort of 'we-ness' connection, a *Jeong* relationship operates instantly. As such, Koreans emphasise the aspect of *Jeong* in the evolution of interpersonal and emotional relationships between people, developing long-term relations through bonding. A common thought system which underlies *Jeong* and solidifies we-ness is a so-called '*Han* 한 (韓)' philosophy. Here, *Han* means 'one', 'big', 'whole' or 'brightness'.[3] This philosophy of *Han* represents a Korean ideal to become one, reunited and harmonised with others. Naturally, the *Han* philosophy appeared in Korean history each time the nation suffered troubles from within or outside, in order to overcome the pressing difficulties. In human relationships, a *Han* mindset is typically expressed collectively in we-ness and *Jeong*. Consequently, the manifestation of *Jeong* in social frames is primarily through fidelity and devotion, often without overt reasoning or assessment. Interactions between Koreans, whether formal or informal, carry the assumption of engagement and interdependency, and such values as independence and autonomy are estimated or assumed to be less important.

While Koreans consider *Jeong* an essential element in human life, promoting the depth, meaningfulness and richness of personal relations, life and environment,

Jeong-ridden behaviours can easily cause tensions, conflict, dissatisfaction and rage. *Jeong* tends to impose one's own expectation and demand for the other party to respond accordingly, or one decides to live by the expectation of people in *Jeong* relationship against one's desire. Consequently, a personal boundary is easily violated and the personal needs can be constantly disregarded by *Jeong*-related people. Once arisen, *Jeong* rarely dissipates and it results in having a strong attachment that hinders living freely and independently. A *Jeong* relationship devoid of mutual affection or closeness can also provoke *Haan*. *Jeong* can also endanger social relations by siding with insiders while segregating outsiders, thereby splitting in-group and out-group. Nepotism and favouritism are indeed common practice in Korea.

Koreans are likely to go to someone they count on, with whom they are usually *Jeong*-bonded, for counselling or advice. In such a relationship, they readily talk, share, understand and exchange thoughts. Hence, it can be challenging for a Korean to open up to an unfamiliar mental health professional without developing any degree of *Jeong* trust between the two. However, it is also to say that once a relation of *Jeong* is developed with the therapist, psychological and emotional interactions can be very rich, intense and insightful.

Noonchi 눈치

The abundance of *Jeong* exchange in social relations demands Koreans to be highly sensitive to others and to maintaining good interpersonal relationships. Thus, they make greater efforts to ensure a relationship remains unbroken, under any circumstances. The Korean word, *Noonchi*, literally meaning 'measuring with eyes', is a concept that characterises a special interpersonal relationship. It is used in various contexts with subtle differences in nuance. If one has *Noonchi*, it means one has an intuitive capacity to read the mind of another person and react accordingly and appropriately. Here, *Noonchi* refers to a sense that is able to understand the needs or mood of others, or the states of a social situation instantly, based not on what is being said, but on appreciating an underlying communication. This then enables unspoken expectations or feelings to be accommodated. Someone who has fast *Noonchi* will quickly grasp and handle the situation, while a person who has too much *Noonchi* would continuously study other people's countenance, voices, body languages and other cues, and try to adapt to their feelings as much as possible. Someone who shows no sign of *Noonchi* is commonly regarded as being ignorant, negligent, insensitive or immature. If someone gives you *Noonchi*, it means being shown a sign or gesture of representing internal thought; someone without *Noonchi* would not easily capture this cue and message. 'Give *Noonchi*' can also have the additional connotation of an unwelcome look. *Noonchi* exchanged between people refers to delivering a message through indirect and non-verbal communication.

While the terms *Haan* and *Jeong* have become increasingly dated, the term *Noonchi* is still very popular. Having an acute sense of *Noonchi* is regarded as being indispensable to interpersonal relationships, especially any relationship with seniors in the workplace. The proper *Noonchi* helps to avoid or prevent any incident which may cause embarrassment and to keep harmonious relationships. Koreans have the tendency not to explicitly express anything that has the potential to make people or the social atmosphere feel awkward or unpleasant. Thus, the intended meaning of the messages is often not directly verbalised. A person may say 'yes' while the real meaning is 'no', and it is up to one's *Noonchi* to capture the hidden meaning – often relying on the context of interaction for guidance. Not surprisingly, misled *Noonchi* can breed misunderstanding and conflict.

On the other hand, one who has too much *Noonchi* can easily harbour anger and disrespect. Excessive *Noonchi* that keeps one on constant alert, can make one extremely nervous, tense, insecure, anxious and fearful. It can generate clinical manifestations of social phobia and paranoia. Anthropophobia, '*Taein-Kongpo* 대인공포 (TK[4])' in Korean, is considered among Korean psychiatrists to be related to excessive cultural emphasis on *Noonchi*. TK Syndrome is categorised as 'culture-bound' in DSM IV nomenclature, and defined as 'an intense fear that the body, its parts or its functions, displease, embarrass, or are offensive to other people in appearance, odour, facial expressions, or movements'. It is distinguished from social anxiety disorder in terms of these culturally prescribed systems of interdependence. The morbid fear of offending or bringing shame upon others, which results in avoidance behaviour, is typically seen in TK Syndrome.

Heung 흥

Heung[5] is best described as an intrinsic sense of joy. Korean linguistic application of *Heung* has penetrated deep into the daily lives of people as the sentiment of gratification, of fun, excitement and enjoyment. *Heung* plays an essential role in the rise of an intensive emotional experience that includes expressive and radiating behaviours, contributing to the purification of negative emotions. The concept of *Heung* and its related cultural phenomena are already found in religious rites in years BC. The first reference to the Korean Peninsula was made in a Chinese document called '*Weizhi* 魏志'. Written in the third century BC as a sort of geographic and travel narrative, it describes the characteristics of Koreans (then-called 'the people of the Three *Hans*; 삼한족') as people who are optimistic, like to dance, sing and drink; *in May and October they hold memorial ceremonies. All tribes gather together and play day and night. They sing and dance beating a rhythm to their hands and feet.*[6] One of the important purposes of the singing and dancing was to attain mental transcendence and to communicate or unite with deities. Korean culture is indeed often referred to as the culture of '*Umju-Ga-Mu* (음주가무; drinking, singing and dancing)'. In times of hardship, as well as of ease, it is not unusual for Korean people to break out into singing or dancing. *Kut* (shamanic rite) always includes singing and dancing. *Pungmul* (percussion) is played in the countryside to accompany agricultural labour, making working together in groups easier and more enjoyable. For instance, many of the most famous folk songs (*minyo*) were conceived by farm labourers singing while they

Figure 1.1 *Pungmul*, at Naju, 1976

completed their hard day of work. Even traditional funeral services in Korea include singing. Mourners sing requiems as they carry the coffins to the graveyard. *Heung*, as the fundamental phenomenon of communication in traditional culture products, was generally evoked within the context of group interaction, through sharing dynamic activities and emotions.

From the viewpoint of Korean cultural psychology, *Heung* is a culture-specific concept that generates and recovers *Jeong*, and settles and resolves *Haan*. Generally, when *Haan* is resolved, and *Jeong* is recovered, *Heung* shows itself. *Heung* is often stimulated by collective activity. One's *Heung* easily boosts the *Heung* of another, especially within the group in sharing joyful or funny events. As *Heung* and action by *Heung* react with each other, the cheerful emotions of joy, happiness and the demonstration of reciprocal empathy enhance self-expression, sense of unity and self-awareness. It is also *Heung* that instils spontaneity and improvisation into the nature of Korean people, promoting a style of 'here and now' interaction and communication. Koreans are often described as people who, once they get into the mood, usually show no hesitation or shyness in allowing their feelings to explode into jubilation and cheerfulness, through which they experience much comfort. This process of unknotting *Heung* is called *Heung-puri*. It essentially contains three curative factors of spontaneity, improvisation and engagement, and is usually found in emotion-driven activities such as free forms of singing, dancing or playing. *Heung* accelerates *Heung-puri* and is also induced by it. Any sense of sadness and frustration seems easily forgotten during the moments of joy found in such activities. Once *Heung* is boosted, everything will be done voluntarily and with flexibility.

Heung has been seen as a major factor in Koreans surviving their various hardships, helping to turn the darkness of their minds towards brightness, even in the

Figure 1.2 Danwon Kim Hong-Do 'Mudong', around 1789

toughest times. In times of suffering, Koreans usually seek consolation in song and dance, and in collective activities containing a lot of humour and laughter. *Heung* has served not only as the coping mechanism for Koreans but also as the impetus to their rich culture in everyday life and a fundamental source of their potentials. Korean people need *Heung* to work productively and *Heung* is also what makes them work proactively. In the presence of *Heung*, Koreans most spontaneously move into action and have a good communication by exchanging *Heung*.

The traditional cultural artefacts such as *samul-nori* (percussion music play) which remains very popular with Koreans today, are intrinsically *Heung*. The Korean mindset and culture of *Heung* has also produced an enthusiasm for creative therapy such as music, art, drama and dance-movement therapy. Because of this notion of *Heung* that is uninhibited and contagious, Korean people usually work better together: *Heung* has been, perhaps, the main reason for Koreans responding so warmly to group therapy rather than to individual therapy.

Korean pensées

Korean thinking has been strongly influenced by four main streams of religious and ethical experience: Shamanism; Buddhism; Confucianism; and Christianity.

These have developed and co-existed in harmony reinforcing one another: Shamanism has built beliefs that human beings are an indispensable part of nature, and need to learn to live in harmony with the ways of nature; Buddhism has influenced Koreans' attitudes and practices of benevolence and compassion towards all living creatures; Confucianism has imbued the codes of ethics for proper thoughts and behaviours; Christianity has catalysed the modernisation of knowledge and of social systems.

Today in Korea, there is neither an official, nor a dominant religion and Koreans enjoy freedom of choice in beliefs. The birthdays of both Buddha and Jesus are equally celebrated as national holidays. A sophisticated mixture of Shamanism, Buddhism, Confucianism, Christianity and other religious elements lives in the Korean subconscious and consciousness and continues to influence the distinctive nature of the Korean mentality. In Korea, *Jong-Kyo* 종교, the term for religion, started being used in the 1900s. Before the terms *Mu-Kyo* (Shamanism), *Yu-Kyo* (Confucianism) and *Bu-Kyo* (Buddhism) became popular, they were called instead *Mu-Do*, *Yu-Do* and *Bul-Do*, terms which stressed the aspect of *Do* (도; *Tao* 道) – a 'Way' that one needs to learn and practise. Hence, it may be more appropriate to understand each pensée not solely from a religious viewpoint but rather from each spiritual, ethical and social-cultural perspective, considering the factors concerned with the ways of thinking and consciousness.

***Shamanism* 무교**

As the earliest and indigenous religion, Shamanism has been a profound force in Korean culture. It embodies thousands of years of their life, thoughts and experiences. Korean shamanism has experienced extended and comprehensive interaction with Buddhism, Confucianism and Christianity and has still survived, successfully integrating with other religions. The influence of Shamanism over the lives of Korean people was so deep that newly introduced beliefs had to comply with certain elements of Shamanism for Koreans to accept them readily.

Belief and ethics

The fundamental belief of Korean Shamanism is that human beings are the essential part of nature and closely interrelated with the ways of nature. In this sense, every human life is best sustained when it adheres to the rhythm and balance of nature. Conversely, if one lives against the flow of the rhythm of nature, life becomes a struggle. As Korean Shamanism is grounded on poly-demonism or polytheism, it does not acknowledge a dualism of human being and god. Since there is no dichotomy between good and evil, human beings are free of dualistic obsessions in their thoughts, more significantly of a hierarchy of human conditions. Dualism is also denied in shamanistic ethics. A wrong in one situation is not necessarily wrong in another; every deed is evaluated within its particular context considering circumstances. Korean Shamanism also recognises no salvation or punishment in the afterlife. By the flow of nature, every human being goes to another place after death by 'turning the corner' and simply lives another life. Hence, there is no notion of a transcendent state of human existence. Naturally, Korean Shamanism facilitates a life in the present life – a worldly existence. This emphasis on the life led here and now is a remarkable feature. The beliefs and ethics of Korean Shamanism, essentially open and relative, concentrating on links with nature and existence in the present, have become impregnated into the basic thinking of all the subsequent Korean pensées.

Interpersonal relations

The preoccupation with a worldly life can lead to a tendency to focus on attaining one's desires now, by any means. Although it may contribute to making Koreans swift, flexible and better adapted to survive, it also provokes a purpose-oriented disposition, egoism and nepotism. Nepotism well defines Korean shamanistic interpersonal relationships. Within the category of family, relative or friend, there is no clear distinction between oneself and another, and their lives are closely intertwined. In such interpersonal relations, one's perceptions and feelings continuously overlap with those of other people. Cohesion and emotional involvement are the essential elements of such a phenomenon, while imprudent intrusion into the affairs of others or a strong display of emotion is considered natural, even ethical. Consequently, the emotional reaction usually felt after the withdrawal of one's affection or exclusion from one's regard, is a particularly strong and prevailing emotion among Koreans. Such shamanic spirit in interpersonal relations naturally corresponds to the notions of *Jeong*. As Korean Shamanism is preoccupied with one's present life and with immediate surroundings, the downside is to have little consideration for public morality and a feeble sense of consciousness for metaphysical values such as ideologies, ethics or philosophies.

Today, belief in Korean Shamanism is not as widespread as it once was, and it is now more a symbol of indigenous culture and a valuable folk tradition. Nevertheless, shamanistic views are still very much part of Korean traits and impact on their thoughts and behaviours, as well as their cultural practices. When traditionally minded Koreans are inexplicably sick, worried about certain things, have a run of bad luck in business, or have mental illness in the family, many of them, whether Christian or Buddhist, still flock to consult a shaman for ways of solving their problems. The expansion of mental health treatment facilities since the late 1980s has not replaced Shamanism. Many contemporary Koreans exhibit shamanic-based inclination towards a human nature that is generally relative, flexible, free, emotional, impetuous and presocentric.

Buddhism 불교

Buddhism arrived in Korea around 372 when a Chinese monk brought Buddhist statues and texts. It was readily assimilated into the indigenous Shamanism

Figure 1.3 Bojo-Jinul 보조 지눌 (1158–1210): Seon master in the twelfth century introduced three profound gates as the methods to cure the diseases: the first gate is to understand the highest scriptural teaching, thus 'theory' as conceptual knowledge; the second gate is to forget the theory, focusing on 'here and now' through Seon dialogue, i.e., the perception of 'outer reality'; the third and most profound gate is complete silence. This aims at the perception of 'inner reality'

producing a unique form of Korean Buddhism. Today, the peaceful co-existence and co-prosperity of Shamanism and Buddhism can be observed in Korean Buddhist temples that set aside a shrine sacred to the high sprits of Shamanism. The shamanistic view of worldly life has influenced Korean Buddhism, while the dualistic idea of paradise and hell, as well as the notion of punishment, was partly absorbed into the shamanistic beliefs through Buddhism. Beyond its religious stance, Korean Buddhism flourished and grew into a major cultural, social, intellectual and spiritual force producing numerous Buddhist books and cultural artefacts and, above all, became actively engaged in social activities. It has played an integral part in the moral and spiritual life of Korean people.

Three distinct features: Hoguk, Tong, Bosal

From early in its history, Korean Buddhism has been drawn to secular elements and earthly prosperity, reflecting the pressing needs of the people of a peninsula repeatedly threatened by invaders and natural calamities. Historically, Korean Buddhism took a prime role in guarding the country. This produced the concept of '*Hoguk Bulkyo* 호국 불교 (State-Protection Buddhism)', a special aspect in the development of Korean Buddhism. Whenever there was a national danger, Buddhist monks were always the first to rise and fight to protect the country. They were always actively involved in social issues and political movements. With this conviction, Korean Buddhism has been a force that brought Koreans together – to create Korean solidarity. Concepts of peace, harmony and unity of all sentient beings, which Korean Buddhism also strives for, became foundations of patriotism.

The second distinct characteristic of Korean Buddhism is the concept of '*Tong Bulkyo* 통불교 (Buddhism of Interpenetration)'. Korean Buddhism successfully overcomes ideological division or conflict by embracing all Buddhist doctrines without predilection for any school or sect. The underlying position is that all different doctrines have the same origin and destination and, regardless of schools, Buddhist thoughts or ways of ascetic practice can remain united or in harmony without strife. Likewise, all beings co-originate and are bound to co-exist through interpenetration. Korean people who mostly prefer to emphasise similarities rather than discrepancies should be indebted to this feature of Korean Buddhism. The spirit of *Tong Bulkyo* has certainly served as an instrument to develop tolerance for different religions or spiritual practices, allowing harmonious co-existence and flexible cooperation. It may also be true that the same holistic and universal approach facilitated an overflowing of varied beliefs and the hovering between religions.

The third central trait of Korean Buddhism is the practice of the spirit of Bodhisattva. A Bodhisattva is an ordinary human being who directs their attention and behaviours to practising the way of life of Buddha. Benevolence is considered

Figure 1.4 Rock-carved Bodhisattva in half lotus position (신선암마애보살반가상) at Sinseonam Hermitage in Gyeongju, around the eighth century © 2011 Eggmoon

the most important quality on the spiritual path to becoming a Bodhisattva. A truthful Bodhisattva is someone who helps all other beings with vigour and patience in perfect benevolence, compassion and wisdom. This status of Bodhisattva can be obtained by anybody irrespective of social status – it is entirely free from discrimination. The spirit and way of being a Bodhisattva certainly influenced Koreans towards an egalitarian and humanitarian orientation. Practically, any Korean who practises Buddhism is now called a Bodhisattva, a '*Bosal* 보살' in Korean.

Today, Korean Buddhism is mostly represented by *Seon* 선 (禪 Zen; meditative state) – known for its stress on meditation, monasticism and asceticism. At the same time, Korean Buddhism has a strong link with communities and society, having always had a clear social responsibility, caring for the suffering and problems of others prior to pursuing personal salvation or enlightenment. It remains a dynamic and influential voice in Korean culture and society today, actively expressing its opinions on issues ranging from human rights, democratisation and social welfare, to environmental protection and political reunification. More and more contemporary Koreans striving for freedom and equality are inspired by its guidance and leadership in fighting against political and social autocracy and injustice.

Confucianism 유교

Critical of both Shamanism and Buddhism, Confucianism became the leading spirit and instrument of a social, political and ethical ideology of the new kingdom of the Joseon Dynasty (1392–1897). Differing from the other traditional styles of thought, Korean Confucianism adhered to very clear and strict moral precepts and codes of conduct thoroughly observed by each individual. Its ideal man was a moral being who lived by the Confucian codes of ethics and behaviours in accordance with a prescribed place in society. On the other hand, Korean Confucianism embraced traditional practices of worshipping spirits of the dead by holding memorial rites for family ancestors, usually on the anniversary of their death. These ancestral rites still remain an important part of Korean life, faithfully observed.

From the viewpoint of Korean Confucianism, a life is simply the course of diligently following through a number of roles. Filial piety (*Hyo*) and loyalty (*Choung*) are the most basic duties one must fulfil. Propriety (*Ye*) means to carry out a role with respect and modesty acknowledging the difference between the self and another, and thereby maintaining interpersonal relationships in harmony and keeping social order intact. Benevolence (*In*) is the essential virtue of guiding the conduct of Confucian interpersonal relationship. It is cultivated within oneself through constant study, along with the display of *Hyo*, *Choung* and *Ye* to other people. A true and genuine man, according to Confucian thought, is thus someone who achieves '*In*' within family, and then also for the community and country.

Vertical relationship: Hyo 효, Choung 충

In Confucian society, the value of an individual's life is secondary to the achievement of '*In* 인 (仁; benevolence)'. The Confucian belief is that the relationship between a parent and a child is the absolute, most important relationship and so a virtue of '*Hyo* 효 (孝; filial piety)' forms the foundation of *In*. It is a child's duty to remain always respectful and totally obedient to their parents and grandparents. This pattern of deference is extended to govern relationships between elder and younger, between ruler and ruled and between husband and wife. *Hyo* also has to be shown towards the dead, as well as the living. The same respect and obedience is expected to be paid to anyone with authority in whatever social circle, whether teacher, boss or leader. Another word for this is '*Choung* 충 (忠; loyalty)' defined as a virtue of one's moral commitments to surroundings and communities as a whole. The social and political dimension of Korea is commonly based on the virtue of *Hyo*, and their leaders hold de facto parental authority over the individual.

Since the values of *Hyo* and *Choung* are central in finding the true meaning of one's existence, personal will usually defers to the will of the family or community; personal decision-making and goal-focus are mostly guided, adjusted and achieved within the expectations of family or community prosperity. Such convention has often undermined relationships through the principal stress on obedience rather than affection, loyalty instead of righteousness. Moreover, it has worked to hinder Koreans from developing the concept of self as an autonomous and independent being; instead, promoting the tendency of constantly seeking recognition or approval and assessing one's place and position in relation to other

Figure 1.5 *Jesa* © 2006 pcamp: *Jesa* is a ceremony commonly practised in Korea – a memorial to the ancestors. It is usually held on the anniversary of the ancestor's death. In most families, this ancestor ritual still remains an important part of their lives and they are faithfully observed

authorities. Nevertheless, the Confucian-adhering individual may not necessarily feel deprived of personal identity, rights or interests, but instead feel supported, stable and secure.

It is still easy to perceive the influence of Confucianism on Koreans today. Younger people are expected to serve and respect older people and not to oppose parents' wishes or the community's will. Despite considerable transformation through the process of modernisation, it is still not hard to observe Koreans' emotional attachment to kindred and family cohesion, which remain as central instruments of a secure life. It is unquestionable that the virtues of *Hyo* and *Choung* have helped to deter family breakdowns in the individualistic climate of modern society. The greatest influence of Korean Confucianism is that human beings depend on others for their existence and one's life cannot exist in isolation.

Education and formality: Ye 예

Another important way to attain '*In* 인' is through constant study and performance of '*Ye* 예 (禮)'. Originally meaning 'sacrifice', the term '*Ye* 禮' was used for any ceremony or courtesy performed at court, and then extended to mean what is ethical and morally right. '*Ye* 예' is now translated as 'propriety' or 'rules of proper behaviour' and embodies the entire range of interaction. *Ye* is comprised of detailed codes of thoughts and behaviours assigned to each person according to one's place in community. Confucius considered proper behaviour, albeit artificial, to be an assurance that everything is seen to be right in its proper place, contributing to preserving morals and trust within the community, and engendering social harmony.

As a code of ethical discipline, *Ye* is learnt and practised through education and study – something also viewed as being part of *Ye*. Learning and studying is regarded as the ultimate conduit through which one could become a fully respectable person. In Confucian belief, one has to be educated to become a righteous person who then serves their community. In Confucian understanding, a more educated person is, almost literally, a better person. Confucian institutions like *Hyanggyo* and *Seodang* and the '*Kwakeo* 과거 (National Civil Service Examinations)' systems were designed to regulate social mobility, and to foster ethical people, who would work to improve society and the nation. Throughout their history, Koreans have attached great significance to education and it became the highest priority for a Korean family and a norm in society. While it places heavy emphasis on self-cultivation as both the object and process of Confucian life through education, Korean Confucianism, however, failed to apply such principles to all people. Being only applicable to aristocratic men, it excluded both women and lower classes. It built a strictly authoritarian bureaucratic society dominated by Confucian political elites. While it raised Korean academic standards, Korean Confucianism cannot avoid the criticism of it promoting intellectual enhancement in favour of ethics and ideology. It firmly excluded foreign knowledge and civilisation. Moreover, it hindered the development of a genuine sense of self by excessive, empty formality, thereby creating a façade of unity, and above all making inequality in Korean society a permanent social ill.

Under the broad spectrum of *Ye*, acts and routines of daily life carried out knowingly or unknowingly are today composed of *Ye* naturally exerted by internalised modes of 'proper' behaviours. The fundamental frame of Korean people, especially for their moral and interpersonal behaviours, is still bound by Confucian concepts. Certainly, the study and performance of *Ye* has produced hierarchical structures while at the same time promoting conflict-avoidant relationships. One who fails to maintain the complex Confucian codes in every relationship is threatened by a fear of shame and loss of face.

Face saving: Chemyeon 체면

Chemyeon 체면 (體面; Social face) literally means presenting a decent countenance to other people. It is a social face closely attached to shame feeling. Excessive consciousness and alertness to the possibility of shame produce a face saving culture. In Confucian belief, you are defined according to your place and position in relation to other people and how they perceive and esteem you. Behaviour, thus, depends on how others perceive it rather than how it is perceived by oneself. Inexhaustibly, a person tries to measure how their acts and thoughts might be viewed through other people's eyes. One who succeeds in keeping *Chemyeon* up is able to consistently behave in accordance with the codes of *Ye*. *Chemyeon* certainly contributes to making Korean people extremely self-conscious and a reason why they are so concerned with appearance over substance, justification over benefit, reputation over condition. It often results in fostering empty formalities and vanity. As one always tries to save *Chemyeon*, external behaviour often does not correspond to the inner mind. The natural expression of emotion is usually hindered under artificial norms and one progressively becomes indifferent to true emotion. The notion of *Chemyeon* has pervaded all aspects of interpersonal relationship. Korean people's awareness of each other's *Chemyeon* is typically so strong that it often results in behaviour that is contrary to people's true self and authentic mind.

Gender and sexuality

Confucianism understands the relationship between man and woman as the foundation of any human relationship and the beginning of all creation. *Ye* between them is considered the most important. Nonetheless, in the name of mutual respect and harmony, Korean Confucianism, openly displays differentiation and discrimination in favour of men. Women who enjoyed a great deal of social and economic freedom during the pre-Confucian period, were reduced to an existence to serve and obey in every aspect of interpersonal relationships. Korean Confucianism holds the feudalistic convention of regarding men as superior to women. A woman is bound to obey the father in childhood, the husband during marriage and the son in old age. A woman's goal in life is simply to become a good wife, a wise mother – a submissive wife and sacrificial mother in the light of *Ye*. Each of these roles is meticulously listed with a series of specific duties and heavy responsibilities. Korean Confucianism implanted a patriarchal family structure and permanent inequality in the relationship between men and women.

Based on the theory of *Yin-Yang*, Korean Confucianism makes a distinct difference between the sexual identities and roles of men and women. Generally, Confucianism regards one's sexual impulses or feelings as something to be suppressed, considering it a deterrent factor for the cultivation of morality. In Confucian society, the sexuality of women is limited to the biological role of child birth, while men can more freely pursue their sexual desires. Women should remain chaste before marriage and they are obliged to live a life of chastity for the rest of their life if widowed. Although the sexuality of women has become comparatively open today, it is still bound to men and their sexual drives.

Today, the basic beliefs of Confucianism have permeated all levels of Korean life and are still shaping Korean society. Korean Confucianism is mostly appreciated for its contribution to family cohesion, community solidarity, respect to elders, moral consciousness and ardour for study. However, its heavy bias towards men, aristocrats (*yangban*) and one's elders and the exceptional stress on formality in relations have held back the mature development of individuals, let alone of society and the nation.

Christianity 기독교

The history of Korean Catholicism begins with the Neo-Confucians' study of Western science in the seventeenth century and throughout the mid-eighteenth century, which evolved into a practising Catholic faith. While Korean Catholicism attracted attention through the efforts and sacrifices of their missionary work, Korean Protestantism emerged in the late nineteenth century developed by the favour of the Korean government and the general public through their activities in education and health care.

Historically, Koreans worshiping a 'Heaven' call it by either *Hanul-nim* 하늘님 (the Heaven) or *Hana-nim* 하나님 (the One). These appellations were tactfully hijacked by the first missionaries by translating God as *Hana-nim*. The primary spiritual principle of Korean Shamanism that is 'respect heaven and love people[7]' is also practically identical to Christian values. There is also an analogy between Christianity and Korean Confucianism on the emphasis of ethics and filial piety. *Hyo* (filial piety) representing the most fundamental virtue and ethical code of Korean Confucianism is simply reflected in the relations between God and a Christian as a father and son relationship.

Clearly, Koreans' traditional understanding of heaven as an absolute power governing all living creatures and the world facilitated the rapid absorption of Christian theology. Traditional beliefs and practices of Shamanism and Confucianism were successfully assimilated into Christianity, and it grew into a unique form of Korean Christianity further reshaping Korea as a politically, economically and socially modern country.

Modernisation

Korean Protestantism was instrumental in implanting modernisation in Korea, not only in terms of introducing advanced scientific knowledge and skills, but also through enlightening the public to ideas of gender equality, justice and freedom. Most of all, Korean Protestantism played a vital role in opening up access to education for women and commoners, who had been oppressed under Confucian society. These groups quickly became enthusiastic advocates of Christianity and more actively involved in social and political reformation. Significantly, Korean Protestants have also inspired independence, pro-democracy and unification movements.

The liberating message of Christianity appealed to many Koreans – liberation from poverty, inequality and class and gender discrimination. It is certainly embedded into *Donghak*, the first indigenous philosophy, viewed by many followers as a political ideology. A leading *Donghak* Peasant Revolution, in 1894, rose up against corrupt officials and an unjust social system. In 1919, Korean Christianity also provided support for the March 1 Movement, a massive public march displaying Korean resistance against the colonial government. Throughout its history, Korean Christianity has always been at the forefront of political and social democratisation movements.

Between 1886 and 1910, Christian missionaries inaugurated at least 750 schools around Korea. From literacy to rational scientific thinking, their teaching covered a wide range of study and applied knowledge. Identifying it with modernity,

Figure 1.6 Jandaehyun Church, at Pyungyang, 1900

the Korean Confucian emphasis on education was certainly a promoting factor contributing to the success of the early evangelisation of Koreans.

Emphasis on worldly life and faith-healing

Korean Christianity grew rapidly in and around churches. One of the major traits of Korean Christianity is its focus on the imminent wishes and rewards achieved through praying, spreading gospels or making offertory. This aspect is very close to the shamanistic belief that luck can be obtained by praying to Heaven. Here, luck means gaining whatever is wished for in this worldly life. In the view of Korean Shamanism, one's life is a given fate and everything in life depends on Heaven's will. Such belief has driven Koreans to be more oriented towards resolving immediate needs and seeking instant gratification instead of self-introspection and making greater efforts for change. Korean Christianity echoes this same worldly and fatalistic outlook. Whether for health, marriage or material success, Korean Christians appeal to God's blessing and good grace through faith and prayer.

Elements of shamanistic rituals and Confucian ceremonies for ancestor worship are also reflected in Korean church services. As with the people's belief in the magical power of shamans, Korean Christians put their faith in the miraculous healing potential of the clergy. Many Korean pastors perform Christian exorcism rituals and faith-healing at revival services. Rather than the personal and profound practices of Christian doctrines and beliefs, Korean Christians tend to regard highly the empowering worship services led by charismatic pastors. Just as Shamanism attaches importance to bodily experience of spirit and ecstasy, Korean Christians believe that they can be in communion with God by fervently singing, clapping and dancing, or through wailing-like prayer during the service. Moreover, the traditional patriarchal family system and unquestionable obedience to one's father or a leader based on the ethical code of Confucian *Hyo* (filial piety) can be also traced to Korean Christians' espousal of faith-healing. One distinct feature of Korean Christianity is the huge number of prayer centres or retreats around Korea. Initially built deep in the mountains in order to lead a religious life while avoiding Japanese oppression, they later emerged as prayer centres and function as places for training, public meetings, revival services or church community retreats. Today, many prayer centres are criticised for degenerating into profit-making places, exploiting the mentally ill or the disabled. Some are run illegally, produce social problems related to pseudo-medical practices or healing operations, and have been exposed for various human rights abuses.

Notes

1 'It is concerned with the way the self is moulded by the social world, in which individuals and groups participate in the construction of their perceived social reality, resting upon

taken-for-granted Knowledge'; extracted from Choi, S. C. & Han, G.S (2000). Psychology in Korea. In A. E. Kazdin (Ed.), *Encyclopaedia of Psychology* 4, (456–458). New York, NY: Oxford University Press.

2 He published 'Korean Psychology' (2000) and co-edited 'Individualism and Collectivism' (1994) and 'Psychology of the Korean People' (1995).

3 When it is positioned in front of other words, it means one, same, much, intense, together, peak and best. Among them, *Han* is used for expressing important concepts like '*hana*' ("one"), '*han-gul*' (Korean alphabet), '*hana-nim*'(God), '*Han-guk*' (Korea), and '*hanul*' (heaven).

4 TK stands for the fear (*Kongpo*) of interpersonal relations (*Taein*). Morita first described TK (對人恐怖 Taijin Kyofusho in Japanese) in the 1930s.

5 Xing (興) first appeared in 'The Analects of Confucius (논어, 論語)' in which the essays about Xing (興) appeared many times such as 'Xing-Yu-Shi (興於詩)' or 'Shi-Ke-Yi-Xing (詩可以興)'. The notion of *Heung*, Xing (興) in Chinese, was first applied in the theory of Chinese poetry as a concept analogous to metaphor or symbol. It was also deeply embedded in the oriental classic art theory as a concept to expose the process of aesthetic experience in creating art and appreciation; extracted from Kim, B. K. (2007). A study of contingency and true heart on Xing (興). *Philosophical Research*, 21, 69–93.

6 The text is extracted from a journal article of Kim, B. K. (2007). A study of contingency and true heart on Xing (興). *Philosophical Research,* 21, 69-93.

7 '*Gyoungcheon-Aein* 경천애인 (敬天愛人)'

Bibliography

Choi, S. C. (1993). Indigenous form of lamentation in Korea, Haan. *Chung-Ang Journal of Social Sciences,* 6, 185–205. [Korean]

Choi, S. C. (1994). Korean Shim-Jeong Psychology. *Chung-Ang Journal of Social Sciences,* 7, 213–237. [Korean]

Choi, S. C., & Han G. S (2000). Psychology in Korea. In A. E. Kazdin (Ed.), *Encyclopaedia of Psychology Vol. 4.* (456–458). New York, NY: Oxford University Press.

Choi, S.C., & Kim, K. (2003). A conceptual exploration of the Korean self in comparison with the Western Self. *Contribution in Psychology*, 42, 29–42.

Hwang, I. K., & Kim, K. H. (2002). Confucianism and mental health in Korea. *Journal of Korean Psychoanalytic Societ*, 13 (2), 146–152.

Kim, Andrew E. G. (2000). Christianity, Shamanism, and Modernisation in South Korea. *Association for Religion and Intellectual Life*, Spring-Summer.

Kim, B. K. (2007). A study of contingency and true heart on Xing (興). *Philosophical Research*, 21, 69–93. [Korean]

Kim, C. L. (2011). A pathological comparison and counselling-alternative idea of Haan and Complex. *Theology & Praxis*, 28, 471–509. [Korean]

Kim, Luke I. C. (1996). Korean Ethos. *Journal of Korean-American Medical Association*, 2 (1), 13–23.

Kim, Luke I. C. (2012). *Beyond the battle line: The Korean war and my life.* Bloomington, IN: Xlibris Corporation.

Lee, S. C. (2011). Revisiting the Confucian norms in Korean church growth. *International Journal of Humanities and Social Science*, 1(13).

Lee, S. H. (1993). *Anthropophobia.* Seoul: Iljogak. [Korean]

Min, S. K. (2008). Clinical correlates of Hwabyung and a proposal for a new anger disorder. *Psychiatry Investigation*, September 5(3), 125–141.
Min, S. K. (2009). Hwabyung in Korea: Culture and dynamic analysis. *World Cultural Psychiatry Research Review*, 4 (1), 12–21.
Min, S. K., & Lee, H. Y. (1986). A diagnostic study on Hwabyung. *Journal of the Korean Medical Association*, 29, 653–661. [Korean]
Oak, S. D. (2010). Healing and Exorcism: Christian encounters with Shamanism in early modern Korea. *Asian Ethnology*, 69(1), 95–128.
Park, H.S. (2007). The substance, history & future of Confucianism in Korea. *The Study of Eastern Philosophy*, 50, 113–127. [Korean]

2 Korean philosophy

While never at the centre of Korean history, Korean Taoism is, nonetheless, what underlies all the traditional Korean pensées. It is the innermost core of Korean mental geography. Korean Taoism is deeply immersed in the Korean indigenous philosophy of *Pungryu* whose central value is the naturalness usually associated with spontaneity and creativity and the *Han*-seeking national spirit described as the primordial state of all things. Both *Pungryu* and *Han* (oneness) stem from the indigenous concept of *Cheon-Ji-In*.

Cheon-Ji-In 천지인

Cheon-Ji-In is the triad of Heaven–Earth–Human as 'One': *Cheon* 천 (天) is heaven; *Ji* 지 (地) is earth; *In* 인 (人) is a human being. Heaven means the spiritual dimension of existence; Earth symbolises the material dimensions of

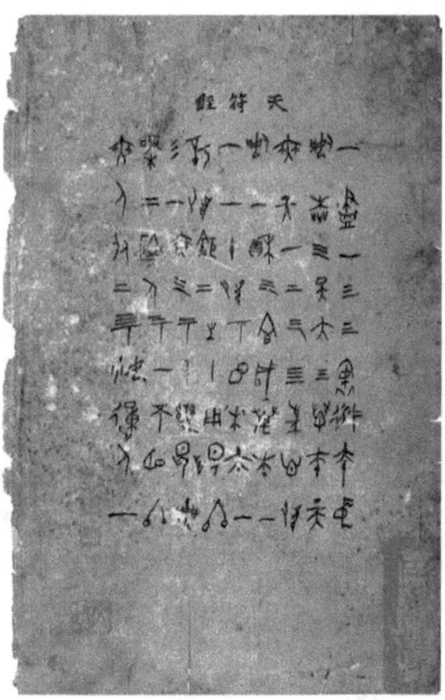

Figure 2.1 Cheon-Bu-Kyung: an example found in the posthumous collections of Nongeun Jo Won-Kil, a scholar of the late Goryeo Dynasty (around 1328–1392)

existence; and Human being represents every form of life and the energy or vitality that animates the life-forms. The concept derives from the oldest Korean scripture *Cheon-Bu-Gyung* (천부경; The Scripture of Heavenly Code). It is presumed to have been orally handed down until the period of 'Baedal' (3898BC–2333BC of ancient Korea) when it was first put into writing in 81 'Nocdo' characters. Nocdo is one of the ancient writing systems in which each letter resembles a pattern of deer hoof prints. The contemporary version in Chinese letters became known when Choe Chi-Won, a scholar in the Silla Dynasty (57BC– AD 935), found the scripture on a tombstone and translated it into Chinese characters.

The scripture begins with a character 'One (일; 一)' and ends with 'One (일; 一)'and delineates that everything in the universe begins and ends with One, having no beginning or end. It teaches of the ultimate oneness (*Han* 한) and the triad of Heaven (*Cheon* 천; 天), Earth (*Ji* 지; 地) and Human beings (*In* 인; 人), signifying that they are all connected as parts of the same cosmic harmony, in the Oneness. With each letter containing its own distinct literal or numerical meaning and distinct energy, the *Cheon-Bu-Gyung* (천부경; 天符經) can be interpreted as an expression of mathematics and energy studies, as well as philosophy.

一始無始一 (일시무시일)
One begins without beginning,
*One (一) refers to the ultimate reality that is the origin of all beings.

析三極無盡本 (석삼극 무진본)
Divided to three, the origin is unchanged,
*One, the ultimate reality, divides to three, representing three different dimensions of existence. The origin of these three remains the same One from the beginning to the end.

天一一地一二人一三 (천일일 지일이 인일삼)
One Heaven; Two Earth; Three Human,
*Heavenly Heaven; heavenly Earth; heavenly Human

天二三地二三人二三 (천이삼 지이삼 인이삼)
Each of Heaven, Earth and Human bears Two (Earth) and Three (Human),
*Together with the preceding phrase, it refers to each element forming a triad making nine different dimensions of existence (Earthly Heaven, Humanly Heaven; Earthly Earth, Humanly Earth; Earthly Human, Humanly Human).

一積十鉅無櫃化三 (일적십거 무궤화삼)
One built to Ten finding no container becomes Three,
**Each individuated being, while developing its complete particularity, has in itself the original three basic elements of Heaven, Earth and Human.*

大三合六生七八九 (대삼합육 생칠팔구)
The sum of the big three is Six, and they form Seven, Eight and Nine,
*This refers to the cycles of the Cosmos; 1+2+3=6 or 1x2x3=6 as the basis of life; 6+1=7, 6+2=8, 6+3=9 as a process of life; and 7+8+9=24 as the 24 seasonal divisions in the lunar calendar, the 24 hours in a day. This represents the constriction and expansion cycles of the cosmos that grows, evolves and circulates.

運三四成環五七 (운삼사성 환오칠)
The move of Three makes Four and encircles Five and Seven,
*Four refers to the energy (*Gi* 기; 氣) of four seasons; Five elements of wood, fire, earth, metal and water, from which all material substance in the phenomenal world is composed; Seven minds of joy, anger, sorrow, fear, love, hate and desire. Forming an integrated circulatory system, three (internal) energies flow into four external energies, five elements of physical energy mechanism and seven parts of emotional energy. It teaches the harmony between Heaven, Earth and Human, which produces *Gi* embracing the body and the mind.

一妙衍萬往萬來 (일묘연 만왕만래)
(The way of) One is profound and mysterious, all goes and all comes,

用變不動本 (용변 부동본)
While the form (or application) changes, the origin remains unchanging,

本心本太陽 (본심 본태양)
The ultimate mind is originally the eternal light,

昻明人中天地一 (앙명인중천지일)
Revere and brighten the Human that bears Heaven and Earth and makes an integrated whole.
*Once Human beings realise their true nature, realise that Heaven and Earth already exist within, and that each individual is One with the rest of the cosmos.

一終無終一 (일종무종일)
One ends without ending.
*There is no ending to the One.

The scripture refers to the principles of *Han* (oneness) and *In-Nae-Cheon* 인내천 (Human is Heaven), which are essential foundations of all Korean philosophy. Basically, it teaches that human beings can be united as one with the essence of the universe by realising the innate sacred promises of *In-Nae-Cheon*, thereby eventually returning to the source of all life. That source is energy that exists as light, sound and vibration which resonates in such phenomena as 'wind' and 'flow'. *Pungryu* is made up of these two characters; *Pung* 풍 (風) meaning wind and *Ryu* 류 (流) meaning flow. As a fundamental principle and 'ultimate truth', the indigenous concept of *Cheon-Ji-In* is profoundly permeated in every belief and thought of the Korean people. Indigenous Korean philosophies grounded on *Pungryu* and *Han* naturally have all inherited and developed this *Cheon-Ji-In* philosophy.

Pungryu 풍류

Pungryu is essentially a notion of living in harmony or becoming one with nature. It refers to a lifestyle of living naturally like the way 'the wind' (*pung*) blows and 'the flow' (*ryu*) goes, representing a harmonious way of life in tune with nature. As a philosophy aspiring towards nature and harmony, it rejects all sorts of dichotomies and embraces a variety of different thoughts and beliefs. When Buddhism, Confucianism and other non-indigenous thoughts were introduced to Korea, *Pungryu* attitudes and approaches were able to facilitate their local integration without any problem. The philosophical features of *Pungryu* clearly enabled Korean societies not to lean towards any particular religion or ideology, but to gain a comprehensive understanding of various spiritualities and philosophies and to strive for their successful co-existence. *Pungryu* also refers to both aesthetic practice and a spirit of play. It is to enjoy the good things in life such as music, arts and literature while being in a naturally free and easy atmosphere. *Pungryu* encompasses everything there is about fun and enjoyment in Korean culture. Features of *Pungryu* have been found, in ancient times, typically in shamanic ceremonies that celebrate nature through group dancing, singing and playing.

The term *Pungryu* first appeared in the ninth century in an epitaph written by a noted Confucian official, philosopher and poet Choe Chi-Won 최치원 (857BC–?) in the Silla Dynasty (57BC– AD935). This epitaph '*Nanrang-Bimun* 난랑비문', transmitted only as a written record in Volume Four of '*Samguk-Sagi* 삼국사기 (History of the Three Kingdoms, 1145)' during the Goryeo Dynasty (918–1392) says: *there is a profound Way before and beyond Buddhism, Confucianism and Taoism in Korea; it is called 'Pungryu.* Choe Chi-Won explained it with the notion of '*Jeophwa-Gunsaeng* 접화군생 (接化群生)' meaning that one is to interact with every living being including animals and plants, and it is *Pungryu* that enables it. At the time, *Pungryu* was regarded as a way for Koreans to relate to others in solidarity and harmony, while disciplining the body and the spiritual state of mind. From the Joseon Dynasty (1392–1897) through the Goryeo Dynasty (918–1392), *Pungryu* was seen more for its artistic and aesthetic values in poetry, song, dance, drawing and discourse, as a tasteful attitude of life. Gradually, it grew into the ultimate means whereby one could escape the hardships of life and enjoy oneself.

As a foundation for the Korean philosophies and as a natural lifestyle that generates the spirit of play with an emphasis on its meaning in art and nature, *Pungryu* is profoundly embedded in the Korean mind. Representing a philosophy of life in harmony with nature within the national spirit of *Han* (oneness),

Figure 2.2 Choe Chi-Won

commonly referred to as the backbone of Korean mind, *Pungryu* has apparently led Koreans along the path to social awareness of the need for justice and freedom. The philosophies of *Il-Shim* (one mind), *Gi* (matter or vital energy), *Donghak* (Eastern learning) and *Ssial* (seed) in particular are notable illustrations of such aspects of the influence of *Pungryu* throughout the centuries.

Il-Shim 일심

An earlier figure attuned to the spirit of *Pungryu* was Wonhyo 원효 (617–686), one of the most eminent and influential scholar-monks in the development of Korean Buddhist history. When Buddhism reached Korea from China via India, it segmented into various sects. Wonhyo significantly succeeded in reconciling the contentions of the different sects through the concepts of *Il-Shim*.

Wonhyo explained the principle of *Il-Shim* as a sea. Likening it to the rivers that coalesce into one large sea, various sects are bound to return to the Buddha mind. This Buddha mind is based on *Il-Shim* 일심 (一心), that is 'One Mind', an absolute state without discrimination of absolutes: purity and impurity, also life and death, are not seen as two extremes. Only a divided mind leads one to affirm one opinion and refute the opposite or to have a different experience of the same reality. By overcoming a dichotomy of mind, one reaches the ultimate reality of a non-dualistic nature that two opposites are not separate in nature; that is *Il-Shim*.

For Wonhyo, everything in the universe was interconnected within *Il-Shim*. One cannot side with a doctrine or opinion as there is no right and wrong and it is possible to bring the two aspects together. Through the principle of *Il-Shim*, he strived to reconcile and unite opposites. By embracing all schools of Buddhism and also absorbing Taoism and Confucianism, Wonhyo sought to integrate the various doctrines into one cohesive whole. By accepting all that was relative and revealing the absolute that lay within, Wonhyo successfully embodied not only the integration of these three teachings but also the essential notions of *Pungryu*.

From the view of *Il-Shim*, the world of enlightenment does not exist separately from the world in which we live. The secular world can be the realm of absolute truth. Thus, if a doctrine is not applied in the daily lives of human beings, it is lifeless and of no use. Wonhyo stressed that one's words should correspond to actions, and one's mind with practice. While most monks of the time enjoyed an easy and prestigious life in the big temples, Wonhyo remained true to his philosophy. His was a wandering existence, visiting villages and towns. Living a secular life along with the common people, he taught them with songs and dances to facilitate their understanding of his philosophy that whoever purifies their mind is able to attain enlightenment, regardless of age, gender or social class. His simple and approachable teaching led to the popularisation of Buddhism amongst ordinary people. The notion and practical philosophy of oneness and interrelatedness of every living being is central to *Il-Shim* which remains a source of guidance and inspiration for Koreans today.

Gi 기

Korean Neo-Confucians in the sixteenth century exchanged heated debates over the theological relations between '*Yi* 이 (理; 'principle)' and '*Gi* 기 (氣; energy)' and their distinct roles relating to the nature of the human mind and the ways of the universe. During this period, whether advocating *Yi* or *Gi*, more importance was given to scholastic pursuit of ideas and conceptual frameworks with an emphasis on the formulation of moral philosophy and social ethics.

Outside the mainstream Neo-Confucian position separating *Yi* and *Gi*, Seo Gyeong-Deok 서경덕 (1489–1546), whose honorific name was Hwadam 화담 (花潭), integrated *Yi* and *Gi*, placing *Gi* above *Yi*. He became the first Korean to formulate a Korean philosophy of *Gi*. Turning his back on the academic and political milieu of the time and leading a life of a country scholar, Hwadam dedicated himself to unravelling the origin of all existence. Different from the other Confucian scholars who mostly relied on theoretical study, he emphasised gaining knowledge by the study of nature and matter through active, close and objective observation. He considered everything from natural phenomena like candle light, a hot spring or wind to the birth and death of human life, through the cycle of the four seasons. He explored the fundamental within the unlimited frame of space and time. It led him to develop his own philosophical system of *Gi*. For Hwadam, the creation and extinction of all existence is an act of *Gi* that endlessly gathers and disperses. All changes in the universe occur by *Gi* itself. It has a permanent presence and continuously exists in different forms or shapes, like a tree which changes according to the season. Both everything and nothing exist within a permanent circulation of *Gi*. This 'nothing' is not non-being but void, and thus is merely unseen. The metaphysical perspective which makes his philosophy of *Gi* most distinctive is this imperishability of *Gi*.

According to Hwadam, *Gi* is the fundamental substance of the universe that creates and transforms all phenomena relating to both the spiritual and the corporeal. His philosophy of *Gi* teaches that every being affects every other being. Each is related to each other and exists only in relationship with each other. It is the relationship and constant interactions that define a thing or matter and make it what it is. Hwadam called this dynamic activity of the universe '*Gi*'. For him, *Gi* is an actual energy and creative entity, and *Yi* (principle) plays only a supportive role as an element within *Gi*.

His philosophy of *Gi* greatly contributed to the theoretical deepening of Neo-Confucianism in the sixteenth century. Trying to understand Neo-Confucianism from a flexible point of view, he embraced various academic approaches and perspectives different from his own which included Buddhism and Taoism. Naturally, Hwadam acquired many followers and disciples who came from various social backgrounds and diverse political groups. Stressing the understanding of all phenomena through conscientious observation and objective exploration rather than speculation based upon ideological notions and theoretical study, his natural and progressive philosophy succeeded in providing practical ways for social and intellectual reformation. He exerted a significant influence on scholars in his time. His adherents expressed a keener interest in social issues and realistic and experimental approaches to social problems. His philosophy flowered into the 'Practical Learning (*Shilhak* 실학; 實學)', developed in response to the increasingly metaphysical nature of Neo-Confucianism. As a philosophy of change, its influence extended to create an intellectual ambience open and receptive to 'Western Learning (*Seohak* 서학; 西學)' introduced in the eighteenth century. In modern Korean, the character *Gi* contributes to words like *Gi-un* 기운 (氣運; *Gi*-transfer) meaning energy or atmosphere, *Gi-bun* 기분 (氣分; *Gi*-dispense) meaning feeling or mood, *Gi-jil* 기질 (氣質; *Gi*-essence) meaning temperament or tendency. Both ancient and contemporary use of the word *Gi* commonly implies something flowing, dynamic and formless. The essence of *Gi* lies in this constant change and flow that clearly corresponds to the way of *Pungryu*.

Donghak 동학

Donghak (東學; Eastern Learning) was the first indigenous philosophy of Korea. As a leading ideology, it enormously influenced Korean society during its transition to social and political modernisation in the late nineteenth century, by calling for social reform, justice, freedom and egalitarianism. In this regard, *Donghak* was not only a philosophical concept but also an active and participatory movement. It was initiated in 1860 by Choi Jei-Woo 최제우 (1824–1864), whose honorific name was Suun 수운 (水雲), in the midst of colonisation by the Japanese and Westernisation by Christian influence. It emerged as a reaction to the erosion of Korean traditional values and ethics and an ideology to alleviate commoners' suffering from extreme poverty and injustice, aiming to re-establish political stability and social security. Corresponding with the spirit of *Pungryu*, *Donghak* embraced other ideas such as Shamanism, Buddhism, Confucianism and Taoism, as well as Christianity which Suun called *Seohak* 서학 (西學; Western Learning). It is, however, noteworthy that *Donghak* was never formulated as a religion since Suun never systematised it as a doctrine or a belief system. Professor Park Maeng-Su, a *Donghak* specialist, stresses the fact that it is more proper to understand *Donghak* not as an object of spiritual faith but as the concept of *Tao* 도 (道), a way of study that human beings ought to learn and practise, as the term *Donghak* (동; 東; Eastern + 학; 學; Learning) indicates.

In the late nineteenth century in the Joseon Dynasty, the social conditions in Korea were extremely difficult. The country was under constant threat of invasion. The squabbling aristocracy showed little concern for the future of the nation or the suffering of the populace and the social discrimination between the *yangban* (aristocrats) and *sangnom* (commoners) was severe. There was serious political and social decay in the nation where traditional religions had lost their vitality. In search of a new way to rescue the nation and give hope to the people desperately in need of guidance, Suun wandered and meditated all over the country for nearly twenty years. In doing so, he was able to observe the political, social and moral erosion throughout the country. In 1860, he finally achieved a great awakening and began propagating his new understanding. Suun's most prominent teaching was 'man is a welkin'. In this, he meant that every human being was the embodiment of heaven and thus should be respected and revered, not only by others but also by themselves. According to him, the welkin was not only a subject of worship but also the world of everybody's daily life, thus respecting humans was the same as revering the sacred. For over three years, Suun taught about the fundamental dignity and equality of all people. The suffering masses, the peasantry, rapidly accepted his teaching and found in the ideology of *Donghak* a revolutionary new hope. For illiterate farmers, Suun set the *Donghak* texts to music. Suun openly urged his followers to participate in social reform and political resistance. The government then became worried about the possibility of revolts and uprisings and began persecuting his adherents and eventually executed Suun in 1864.

Choi Si-Hyung 최시형

The teachings of *Donghak* were then carried further by the distinguished spiritual leader Choi Si-Hyung (1827–1898), whose honorific name was Haewol 해월 (海月). If the seeds of *Donghak* were sown by the founder Suun, it was Haewol

Figure 2.3 Choi Si-Hyung

who made them sprout and take root into individual and social consciousness. Like Suun, Haewol taught of the fundamental dignity and equality of all human beings, contrasting with the prevailing unjust, discriminatory class system. His main argument was that the distorted relationships between people and nature, between female and male and between mind and body were the fundamental causes of social, political and ecological problems. These relationships could not be overcome by abstract reflection but by dynamic action for change. Even in the midst of persecution by the government, Haewol successfully led the movement, expanding it throughout the country. He spent almost forty years establishing numerous small-scale spiritual communes all around the country. These new communes succeeded in the function of *Hyangyak* 향약 (鄉約), previously created by the local Confucian ruling class to govern local communities. *Donghak*'s grassroots spiritual communes became the first autonomous organisation in the Joseon Dynasty. Nonetheless, this self-induced modernisation could not withstand Japanese colonial power. Haewol was executed in 1898.

Samkyung 삼경

Haewol introduced 'the concept of *Samkyung* 삼경 (三敬; the three honouring)'. *Samkyung* is to honour heaven; honour human; and honour nature (or thing). He proclaimed that, heaven, humans and nature are not independent substances but are of a single, identical substance, and that no hierarchical distinction can be made between them. In a single, undivided universe, the spiritual, the natural and the human simply cannot be separated or contrasted. For him, heaven is life itself and both humans and nature are an embodiment and concrete form of heaven. Everything in the universe is equal to heaven. Thus, to revere heaven is precisely to respect oneself, not only one's mind but also one's body, and all living and inanimate things. *Samkyung* taught that one should awaken one's divine self at every moment and nurture activities in daily life, whether eating food or caring for house or plants, to get into accord with heaven and be united with its spirit. Haewol, thus, emphasised mindful practice in everyday life as a way of honouring heaven, humans and nature. The idea that each person acts autonomously in respect of these three elements was indispensable to the *Donghak* that Haewol advocated. He asserted that one who practises the *Tao* honours heaven, humans and nature: if one honours heaven but not other humans, or one honours humans but not nature, one cannot reach the *Tao*.

Sain-yeocheon 사인여천

Haewol highlighted an important ethical idea in *Donghak*, called '*Sain-yeocheon* 사인여천 (事人如天)'. The literal meaning 'treat man like heaven' implies an ethics that a human is divine in original nature and is not dictated by one's condition, thereby all human beings should be treated with respect, dignity and equality. Challenging all forms of discrimination on the grounds of age, gender or social class in Korean society, it gave ordinary peasants and marginal Confucian intellectuals a sense of worth. In place of the vertical Confucian social system, they initiated a new horizontal structure and mode of life defending the right to equality for all, including women and children. The egalitarianism and humanism of *Donghak* induced a most realistic and empirical reformation at the time and contributed to the nation's independence in later years. Many subsequent popular democratic movements calling for justice, equality, freedom and political reform, albeit different in historical circumstances, must be traced to the *Sain-yeocheon* ethics. As a practical indigenous philosophy, *Donghak* continues to be a genuine resource for the spirit that guides modern Korean society on the path of democratic consciousness.

Ssial 씨알

The spirit of *Donghak* that proclaimed that every human should be treated equally and honoured under heaven was passed on to the *Ssial* philosophy. It originated with Yu Young-Mo 유영모 (1890–1981) who used the term '*Ssial* 씨알', meaning 'seed'. His first use of *Ssial* referring to commoners or grassroots was during his lecture at the YMCA in December 1956. Yu Young-Mo observed that the country had been destroyed by the ideology of the privileged noble class, and spent his life searching for an alternative by seeking to integrate the thoughts of Taoism, Buddhism, Confucianism and Christianity. He attempted to re-conceptualise a Christian understanding of God and equate it with 'Nothingness 무 (無)' or 'Void 공 (空)', with the 'Great Ultimate 태극 (太極)', with the 'One' and with

Figure 2.4 Ham Seok-Heon (left), his teacher Yu Young-Mo (right) © 2008 Ssialsori

'*Tao* 도 (道)'. He proclaimed that a clue for producing such an idea could be found, for instance, in 'the sunburnt face of a farmer'– an ordinary person embodying a nature-friendly lifestyle with great balance of body and spirit, demonstrating harmony between nature and man. Yu Young-Mo believed that these ordinary people should be the master with God's mind and should be served. This formed the foundation of *Ssial* philosophy. By integrating Eastern and Western thoughts, the *Ssial* represented a harmonious and peaceful philosophy pursuing the truth of the 'One'. Yu Young-Mo was known for his abstemious life and his pursuit of knowledge through meditation. He was the first thinker who spoke and wrote about philosophy in modern Korean language.

Ham Seok-Heon 함석헌

Ham Seok-Heon (1901–1989) followed in the steps and faith of his teacher, Yu Young-Mo. He developed *Ssial* into a leading spirit and philosophy of the twentieth century. While Yu Young-Mo coined the term *Ssial* to represent more or less the most vital unit of history, society and life just like the atom is the ultimate unit of matter, Ham Seok-Heon understood *Ssial* to represent the oppressed, marginalised and unprivileged ordinary people who are actually at the centre of society and the source of its life force. Unlike Yu Young-Mo who stressed self-training, meditation and an ascetic life, Ham Seok-Heon actively engaged in various social activities and shared the suffering of *Ssial*.

Called the 'Conscience of Korea' and the 'Prophet in the Era of Suffering' during his lifetime, Ham Seok-Heon was a distinguished historian, philosopher and leader of the fierce movement for democracy in the twentieth century. The initial formation of his philosophy began with the study of Korean history during the 1920s. He first encountered the philosophical Taoism of Lao-tzu and Chuang-tzu through Yu Young-Mo in 1921 at Osan School. Here, Yu Young-Mo had applied his own oriental philosophical interpretation to his teaching, as well as his Christian faith. In the late 1920s, Ham Seok-Heon mostly immersed himself in historical research. He published his views and interpretation of Korean history in the magazine 'Bible and Joseon (성서조선, 1927–1942)' and became known as an aspiring young Korean historian. It was around this period that he began to develop his philosophy.

Denying the historical perspectives of the privileged noble class, Ham Seok-Heon considered the commoners to be the principal actors in Korean history. He proclaimed that it was a history of suffering and the main actor was the *Ssial*. For him, it was sacrifice, resistance or confrontation by unprivileged ordinary people that echoed throughout Korean history. In 1947, he escaped from North Korea and was reunited with his teacher Yu Young-Mo. He attended once again 'Yu Young-Mo's Oriental Study Group' and came to re-appreciate the values of the Eastern classical philosophies. He speculated on the necessity of a new way for *Ssial* and found the cue in the re-interpretation of Eastern philosophies. He was an especially strong advocate for Taoist stress on a way of natural, free, equal and peaceful living, in complete harmony. He regarded it as a guiding principle for a stand against discrimination, unfair restriction and violence. Taoism certainly provided a philosophical foundation and inspiration for the *Ssial* philosophy.

Figure 2.5 Ham Seok-Heon

According to Ham Seok-Heon, in order to lead a true life, one had to pay attention to the *Ssial* and be responsible for the *Ssial*'s sufferings. The *Ssial* philosophy inspired the fight against social injustice and the struggle for dignity, freedom and equality, and encouraged the *Ssial* to strengthen their independent spirit. Above all, it set a high value upon the 'self-acting' of each individual as a responsible and independent being, as well as on the spirit of oneness – to restore wholeness as a single unit. The socio-historical view of *Ssial* philosophy evolved thereafter to become the struggle against unequal and inhuman conditions in Korean society.

Self-acting 스스로 함

Noting that the key to resolving both human and social problems is within oneself, Ham Seok-Heon emphasised 'self-acting'. The main focus of his *Ssial* philosophy was to reinvigorate the oppressed national spirit by this 'self-acting'. To him, to live is to struggle, think and love – to think is to love and to love is also to struggle. These three were united into one and 'self-acting' was the principle that integrated struggle, thought and love by linking body, mind and spirit. He underlined that life in itself necessitates struggle and the nature of life lies in non-violent struggle. The struggle that he proclaimed is not necessarily to fight against the other through fear or hatred, but to overcome one's self by thought and with love as creative 'self-acting' in the pursuit of self-realisation.

For him, an act of love was also defined as a struggle to achieve humanity within the spirit of wholeness. In his view, to love is when one willingly confines one's freedom before that of the other and that only love as a self-confinement can reconcile human beings. Freedom is a capability to autonomously attain love and reach wholeness, therefore, true freedom always stands on interrelationship beyond the freedom of a person's inner struggle. Ham Seok-Heon explained that in order to live a life of self-acting, one requires incessant self-revolution and self-renovation, and presented *Ssial* thought as the philosophy of revolution and renovation of oneself.

Hanism 한 사상

'Wholeness' or 'oneness' is another major theme of his *Ssial* philosophy. Although Ham Seok-Heon did not develop a systematic theory of *Han* 한 (韓; oneness), his thoughts and practices were founded upon the basic understanding of *Han* as peaceful, kind, inclusive and harmonious collective consciousness. He placed *Han* as the national spirit of Korean people at the core of *Ssial* philosophy and made it its ultimate goal. Hanism was the main output of his unique life and spirituality. According to him, the *Han*-seeking national spirit is represented as pacifism which pursues peaceful virtues such as tolerance, compassion and love; it urges the achievement of integration and assimilation. It is also linked with the non-violent resistance he led against socio-political oppression. Furthermore, he believed that the goal of history was for human beings to become one. To him, becoming one is also conceived as the basis of culture and of all religions. Within this spirit, he embraced various Eastern ideologies, religions and moral schools of thoughts, as well as Western philosophies.

By striving to achieve a unity between different thoughts, he finely established open and comprehensive thinking beyond the theories and practices of each ideology or religion, embodied in the *Ssial* philosophy. The oneness of body, mind and spirit that constituted the principle of self-acting integrating struggle, thought and love, was clearly linked to Hanism. Extraordinarily, Ham Seok-Heon himself sought to reach a state of deep spirituality by having one meal per day and examining his inner mind by practising meditation. Based on free extensive thought, removing any prejudice and overt inclinations, he tried to obtain real or true thought, transcendental love and freedom.

Bibliography

Choi, J. M. (2010). The birth of East: focus on Suun Choi Jei-Woo's Donghak and Bombu Kim Jeong-Sol's Dongbanghak. *Journal of Korean Society of Yang-Ming Studies*, 24, 177–226. [Korean]

Ham, S. H. (2009). *Ham Seok-Heon collected works volume 1–30.* Seoul: Hangilsa. [Korean]

Jeong, B. H. (2011). Postmodernism and Korean Pungryu. *Academy of Korean Aesthetics*, 10 (1), 133–164. [Korean]

Jeong, B. J. (2010). *Master Wonhyo, An overview of his life and teachings: Korean spirit and culture VI.* Flushing, NY: Diamond Sutra Recitation.

Kim, B. K. (2010). Hwadam Seo Gyeong-Duk's ecological thought and literature. *Korean Thought and Culture*, 55, 35–60. [Korean]

Kim, S. B. (2009). Ham Seok-Heon and idea of Ssial philosophy. *Journal of Korean Philosophical Society*, 109, 1–27. [Korean]

Kim, S. S. (2002). Ham Seok-Heon and Taoism. *The Korean Cultural Studies*, 2, 91–111. [Korean]

Kim, Y. H. (2012). A study on the public-common philosophical thought in Haewol`s three worship thoughts. *Journal of Donghak*, 24, 7–35. [Korean]

Lee, C. I. (2008). The imperishability of Gi and the spiritual beings. *Journal of Korean Studies*, 31(1), 31–58. [Korean]

Lee, H. H. (2008). Donghak and modernity. *Journal of Korean Association of National Thought*, 2 (2), 9–24. [Korean]

Park, J. S. (2000). Ham Seok-Heon's national spirit and Christian thought. *Korea Journal*, 40 (2), Summer.

Park, M. S. (1994). Establishment of Donghak and its philosophical features. *Lecture on Modern and Contemporary History*, 5, 19–42.

Park, S. J. (2010). Individual and entirety in Donghak thought. *Journal of Donghak Society*, 20, 119–155. [Korean]

3 Folk treatment

Traditionally and historically, the use of arts play for the relief of suffering of body and mind was the most accessible and common in the everyday life of ancient Koreans who exceptionally enjoyed singing and dancing. While arts play itself could be healing, it was often combined with lots of humour and laughter. This feature of arts play was commonly seen in shamanic rites composed of various arts activities. The *Pungryu* spirit and indigenous Korean beliefs on the influence of the spirit upon the material world and illness were deeply infused into shamanic rites and they were particularly sought after for treating the ill mind of traditional Koreans.

During the Three Kingdoms Period (57BC–AD668), Chinese medical knowledge was introduced to Korea by travelling Buddhist monks. The view of traditional oriental medicine that imbalance in the functions of energy or disharmony in interaction between the human body and the environment generates illness was generally adopted as the basic theory of traditional Korean medicine. Some methods found in traditional oriental medicine, similar to modern psychotherapy approaches of supportive, suggestive or didactic technique, were also used. Traditional Korean medicine had its glory days in the Joseon Dynasty (1392–1897). The most distinctive trait of traditional Korean medicine and healing was its human and mind-centred approach in the treatment of illnesses. Its practitioners considered emotions, as well as their lifestyle and personality, to be the major causes of diseases, and stressed mental stabilisation as the curative method. The emphasis on a healthy mind in treating a disease was well illustrated in the two most historically prominent books: *Dongui-Bogam* (Treasured Mirror of Eastern Medicine, 1613) and *Dongui-Susae-Bowon* (The Principle of Life Preservation in Oriental Medicine, 1894), including the '*Sasang-Uihak*', a method whereby people were divided into four constitutional types based on their inherent traits. Those who suffered from exceptionally grave illnesses would try both traditional Korean medicine and shamanistic healing for cure.

Autochthonous practices

Arts play

The spirit of joyful 'arts play' has been historically central to Korean people. Always placed close alongside their daily lives, arts play such as dance, song, drama and music has served as an important outlet for coping with both physical and emotional difficulties. From the ancient rituals to the folk arts, what was essentially communicated through arts play was a sense of relief for pent-up emotions and daily stresses, and of sharing with others in open space and in groups, often resulting in the experience of catharsis. In Korean history, the traces of arts play as an effective instrument that produces *Heung*, resolves *Haan*, and thus creates *Jeong* are not lacking. Without doubt, arts play has been an absolute means of people enduring, resisting and surviving their deep sadness and suffering, however arduous and destitute their lives were.

Foremost in such arts play was mask play, *tal-nori* 탈놀이 in Korean. It is a combination of dance, song and drama. While *nori* 놀이 is a Korean word for play, the word *tal* 탈 meaning a mask was borrowed from Chinese 脫 meaning 'let it go', 'be free' or 'be delight'. *Tal-nori* originated from ancient rituals. In earlier times, it was essentially expressive of the invocation of magical and supernatural powers holding a message of farmers' wish to avoid relentless natural disasters. The first mask excavated is Bangsangssi 방상씨 탈 probably originated in the sixth century of the Silla Dynasty (57BC–AD935). Gradually, the ritualistic aspect of *tal-nori* faded away and further emphasis was given to expanding its dramatic quality. During the Goryeo Dynasty (918–1392), it became an exceptional implement for the general populace to discharge their frustration and daily stresses. It was also an effective tool for the ruled class, whose lives were characterised by social oppression and constraints, to display the social and human conditions they experienced under the injustice and corruption of the time. The especially vigorous dance motion helped the players both to express their feelings of resentment and resistance. While concealing their identity behind a mask, people were free to improvise their roles in a context for self-expression that was normally inhibited or constrained.

Traditionally, the essence of Korean arts play lay in the 'detachment' of oneself from harsh reality, carried out through the sublimated arts form, characterised by great comedic spirit. Korean arts play was historically featured as being self-expressive, spontaneous, joyful and playful. Another remarkable feature was the keen and voluntary participation of people who freely mingled with each other. Within the joyful arts play, Koreans were always dynamic communicators of their emotions. Today, it is not unusual for Koreans under stress to turn to arts of any kind. *Tal-nori* is always one of the most common and sought after arts plays amongst Koreans of all ages together with *samul-nori* 사물놀이 (percussion music play). Such arts play is considered to be one of the most immediate and powerful ways for both physical and emotional release. Both *tal-nori* and *samul-nori* are enjoyed not only as a recreational activity but also in social and political manifestations. They have also been adopted in expressive arts therapy and group therapy. The dynamic of spirit-boosting and treating the ill mind through arts play still exists as a strong undertone of Korean mind. This fundamental grounding for the spirit of arts play is indebted to the '*Suhn* play' of ancient times.

Figure 3.1 Tal-nori

Suhn *play*

Suhn 선 (仙) is a Korean word made up with two Chinese characters 人 (human) + 山 (mountain), literally meaning 'person in (or to) mountain'. Historically, it depicted ancient Koreans' wishes to become one with nature and seek freedom

Figure 3.2 Tal-nori at Andong © 2008 Koreanet Korean Culture and Information Service

and peace of body and mind. In ancient tomb murals, an old man who was considered divine, mature and a free man, frequently appears. Light and easy, he enjoys the landscape while leisurely drinking, playing music or dancing. Such a scene was referred to as *Suhn* play.

In ancient Korean, the character 僊 meaning 'dancing' instead of 仙 was used, suggesting that *Suhn* principally connoted arts play amid pristine nature in particular. As an archetype of arts play, *Suhn* indeed provides a means for understanding the nature of Koreans' exceptional reverence for arts play throughout their history. Fundamentally, *Suhn* play was pursued in an attentive and meditative manner through paying very close attention to breathing while playing arts. It was considered to be an essential way for disciplining the body and the spiritual state of mind. Both ancient scholars and groups of male youths regularly travelled around mountains and rivers and trained themselves through singing and dancing while communing with nature. Naturally, such *Suhn* play was favoured by aristocrats as an important means for self-comfort and self-cultivation, On the other hand, the more dynamic aspect of arts play of *Suhn*, serving the same purpose, was accentuated amongst the general populace.

In *Suhn* play, breathing and meditation were equally essential elements and independently these have been the leading methods by which Korean people trained their bodies and improved their mental state throughout history. This aspect of *Suhn* play certainly contributed to the distinguished development of *Seon* Buddhism and meditation psychotherapy of latter years in Korea. Although the initial form of *Suhn* play shrank to be just a folk belief and gradually faded away, it bore the primary characteristics of Koreans and the most intimate and intrinsic feature of autochthonous practices of Korean people for care of the mind. *Suhn* play has clearly acted as the foundation for their underlying mental energy. In Korean history, arts play and meditation were truly the most accessible means of healing for Koreans to find relief from suffering or ill mind, as well as for self-cultivation of mind and body. The artistic and playing characteristics of arts play adjoined shamanic rites through which shamans helped Korean people to release their suppressed emotions.

Mudang and *Kut*

Shamanism has played a key role as the carrier of Korean life, thoughts and culture. The *Mudang* 무당 (shaman) and *Kut* 굿 (shamanic rites) are two main elements of Korean Shamanism. Traditionally, Koreans would seek the help of the *Mudang* to cope with their sufferings commonly linked with *Haan*. By helping people with their mental or emotional issues and to work them through, notably in the context of entertainment and spectacle including dancing, singing, music and drama, the *Mudang* was comparable to an expressive, family or group psychotherapist, and thereby *Kut* led by the skilful *Mudang* was akin to therapy. Today, many Koreans would still prefer the traditional way of finding solutions within the family, through the *Mudang* and *Kut*, especially when it concerns mental issues. According to the Korea Worshipers Association, there were an estimated 1,000,000 *Mudangs* in 2010.

The Mudang 무당

In Korea, the *Mudang* might be the first and most archaic healer and possibly the forerunner of the modern psychotherapist. Ancient Koreans believed that illness was caused by spirits, which only the *Mudang* could subdue. Regarded as a healer, fortune teller, human cultural asset and refined artist, *Mudangs* who were, in Korea, mostly women were trusted to provide healing on physical, psychological and spiritual levels.

The principle role of the *Mudang* was to play a role as a mediator between spiritual and human worlds through a series of ceremonies. Typically, the *Mudang* would begin the healing process by holding a consultation in regard to the issues that people were facing. She sympathetically listened to their story, and then went on to diagnose the problems, usually attributing them to occurrences in the spirit world, such as an ancestor's ill-will. The solution was to restore the good-will through a ritual called *Kut* and mediation initiated by the *Mudang* herself. With the sense of connection to the good-will restored, the ill-person and his or her

Figure 3.3 Mudang and *Kut* © 2010 Splashman

family would feel reassured that healing had taken place. More fundamentally, however, the *Mudang* would reveal that the main cause of illness or misfortune in the family was a deficiency of giving, care and concern; in other words, an absence of *Jeong* amongst the family members, which resulted in the *Haan*-related illness to the person. The *Mudang* who was generally once sick herself with a mental sickness called 'spirit illness', and had the experience of overcoming and transcending her mental illness and living the *Haan*-ridden life of the oppressed and despised as a women and shaman, would be exceptionally considerate and empathetic towards one's grievances and suffering. The *Mudang* full of empathy or *Jeong* would successfully support the ill-person and the family members to express and release the repressed emotions by openly disclosing their painful and traumatic life events and memories. The charismatic *Mudang* would skilfully instigate them to weeping, mourning, raging or laughing, through deliberately turning to supernatural beings and talking with them, which usually provoked a dramatic and emotionally intense reaction. By persuasion, reassurance and suggestion, but most of all, by encouraging people to participate in dancing and singing, the *Mudang* would stimulate much more to relieve pent-up emotions and *Haan*, and have a cathartic experience. In this regard, the *Mudang* was a successful folk psychotherapy of family, group and expressive arts.

The *Mudang*'s thinking and activities were highly humanistic in attitude and such a humanistic approach was regarded as being very effective. Although *Mudangs* were demonised by Christian missionaries, driven underground during Japanese colonial rule, disparaged as charlatans under the military governments after the Korean War, *Mudangs* have preserved an important tradition and culture of Korean life and still shine in the everyday life of Korean people.

Kut 굿

The Korean Shamanic rite, *Kut* signifies both the therapeutic medium and the therapeutic space through which the healing takes place. It varies according to the regions in which it was performed and the acting and improvisation varies from village to village. Nonetheless, each *Kut* had the same orientation in that it was fundamentally human-centred, focused on this life and highly dramatic and entertaining. *Kut* as a collective ceremony was traditionally carried out to ask for a fortune, worship spirits or cure illnesses. Its principal aim was to create unity by restoring the harmony and balance between the spiritual and natural world and this human life, whereby the misfortune or illness could be resolved.

Kut that is today promoted as 'intangible cultural assets', was commonly composed of dances, songs and music of various traditional folk arts. It provided a medium and space in which a family or group of people freely and voluntarily expressed their emotions and especially exchanged *Jeong* with each other within the context of joyful arts play led by the *Mudang*. This release of *Haan* was the essence of *Kut* that effectively induced the warm feeling of *Jeong* among people through taking part in arts play.

Kut *as expressive therapy*

Kut 굿 always began with highly improvisational music followed by the song and dances of the *Mudang*, vibrating to and summoning the spirits. Bouncing on her toes, swinging her arms, she danced and span whereby the spinning itself was hypnotic. Then, the *Mudang* sang the spirit messages. People gathered around and listened with awe to the words of spirit. At this point, the entertainment and playfulness began. The improvised comedy and satiric characterisation of *Kut* would induce lots of laughter and joy and help to relieve the tension which it created. Commonly, people were invited to participate and they most willingly joined in singing and dancing, each imitating the *Mudang*'s gestures and movements. As *Kut* concluded, people would usually continue to sing, talk and play sharing food and drinks prepared for *Kut*.

Evidently, the primary means of soliciting the good-will of spirit through *Kut* was by entertainment and play itself. Being spontaneous and highly enjoyable, *Kut* including music, dance and mimetic gestures, produced impromptu symbolic dramas in which the repressed feelings were revealed and clarified, thereby the healing was carried out. In *Kut*, people were encouraged to participate in various cathartic activities such as dancing, singing, playing, laughing and weeping, and to interact with signs and symbols representing their desire and problems through arts play. The public dramatical performance of *Kut* enabled people to display even extreme emotions without shame, mostly conveyed without words through the sublimated art forms. With expression and interaction through music, movement and play as the primary forms of communication, *Kut* had several specific

Figure 3.4 Hyewon Shin Youn-Bok 'Munyeo-shinmu', around 1805

characteristics of expressive therapy, i.e., self-expression, active participation, imagination and mind–body connections.

Kut *as family/group therapy*

Kut 굿 was usually carried out for a family. Typically *Kut* for a family was initiated for an individual who fell ill from an unknown cause. Traditional Koreans accepted death as a part of life and they believed that the spirit of the dead whose *Haan* was kept unresolved caused the illness in the family member. In *Kut*, the family's story was acted out and the *Kut* became a space in which the family members could speak out to divulge facts and wrong deeds within the family. It was believed that this process eventually brought the release of *Haan* of the dead and the restoration of the relationship between the family members. At this point, the *Mudang* usually gave the whole family didactic instructions, admonishing mutual cooperation and filial piety, love or compassion, appeased the spirit of the dead to enter into a good place, and announced that peace and prosperity would be with a family. It was also thought that one's illness was caused by the deep attachment of the living to the dead and *Kut* in this sense helped the living to accept the reality that the loved one has died and to cut the attachment through the symbolic ceremony of *Kut*. Should it be for dispelling sickness or mending broken relationship, *Kut* clearly spoke to the family's most immediate need and concern and conduced to deepen and enrich the familial relationship and re-establish wellness.

On the other hand, *Kut* for the village was, above all, a festival for all the community, where villagers could wash away their ill feeling and strengthen their cooperation. In a sense, it was an open group ritual to pray for personal blessing, well-being and safety from disaster. At the same time, it functioned as social action in fulfilling the need of a community and promoting its solidarity. In *Kut*, all villagers mingled together not only sharing food but also dancing and singing irrespective of age, sex or social position. The essence of *Kut* as the psychotherapeutic process was a kind of trance in which participants danced and shared feelings in groups. In particular, the playfulness of *Kut* with lots of humour and laughter offered a sense of liberation from the bondage of misfortune, illness or disaster. It helped to relieve the oppressive feelings and bring vitality into their life. As a collective activity, *Kut* effectively developed a sense of inclusiveness, unity and hope, which again generated joy and liberation.

Kut that was typically filled with gestures, objects and symbols offered an opportunity for the people to encounter their pain and sufferings intermediated by spirits or supernatural beings. The positive function of *Kut* was, after all, to relieve individual anxiety and inner conflict by way of sublimation processes. However, the strong tendency of projection that both the good and the bad of life depend on the will of supernatural beings should be its negative aspect. There was no apparent individual responsibility and all problems were attributed to supernatural causes, which could be resolved through *Kut* mediated by the *Mudang*.

This strong projective tendency is presumably one of the reasons why even today the insightful approach to mental illness is tricky with Koreans.

Folk-psychical approach

Oriental psychical methods

The methods which were traditionally applied in oriental medicine to treat mental illnesses were found in Korean literature as early as the seventh century. These methods are still in practise in Korea where 'Oriental Psychiatry 한방정신의학' is taught and practised, along with other techniques of oriental medicine, at universities and hospitals specialising in Traditional Korean Medicine (TKM).[1] They recognise that the methods they use are similar to modern psychotherapy of cognitive behavioural approaches.

Jieon-Goron *therapy* 지언고론 요법

The first documented case of individual psychotherapy in Korean history is the case of treating the 'depressed' Chungkong, a high official of the Unified Silla Dynasty in 822. *Samguk-Sagi* 삼국사기 (三國史記; History of the Three Kingdoms, 1145)[2] records:

> Chungkong became ill after a hard day of work on appointing government officials. The doctor prescribed him medicine for heart failure. Chungkong said that he was just 'feeling vague and uncomfortable (혼묵묵 정신불쾌이; 昏嘿嘿 精神不快耳)'. A Confucian scholar named Nokjin who recognised the nature of his illness told him that his disease could be cured by 'proper words and high discourse (*Jieon-Goron*)'. Finely appealing to the reason and the knowledge of Chungkong, Nokjin held discourse bringing persuasion and making suggestion. After a few meetings with him, Chungkong felt relieved and told others that listening to Nokjin, it was like a medical treatment.

The term *Jieon-Goron* therapy (至言高論療法) is found in Hwangei-Naekyung (黃帝內經; The Yellow Emperor's Classic Work on Internal Medicine), a Chinese medical book from around 200BC. It was elaborated in *Dongui-Bogam*, a Korean medical encyclopaedia printed in 1613. *Jieon-Goron* literally meaning 'proper words, high discourse' was to encourage regaining the self through the ways of assurance, persuasion and suggestion. *Jieon-Goron* therapy is widely used even today by the TKM psychiatric specialists. It is a talking therapy in which the patient who feels cared for, understood and reassured, can become relieved from negative feelings and symptoms and regain the self. *Jieon-Goron* therapy corresponds to supportive, didactic or suggestive psychotherapy.

Yijung-Byunqi *therapy* 이정변기 요법

Samguk-Yusa 삼국유사 (三國遺事; Memorabilia of the Three Kingdoms, 1281)[3] tells the story of Gyungheung, a Buddhist monk during the days of King Sinmun (681–692, Silla Kingdom). He suddenly fell ill and suffered for a month. A Buddhist nun came to see him. She said; 'A good friend can cure an illness 선우원병설 (善友原病說) …. For your illness is caused by worries 우로소치 (憂勞所致), it can be cured by laughter and joy 희소가치 (喜笑可治).' She prepared comical dances in eleven different masks, which was 'hilarious' as described. While he was laughing hilariously, he was cured without realising it.

What was depicted as a method to cure the illness of Gyungheung is displacement of the worries through turning to something funny and joyful. This is what is called *Yijung-Byunqi* therapy (移精變氣療法) derived from Hwangei-Naekyung. *Yijung-Byunqi* literally means 'displace *Jung* 정 (精; body essence and sexual energy), alter *Gi* 기 (氣; life force)'. Through displacing or dispersing mental activity focused on illness-related thoughts, *Yijung-Byunqi* therapy aims to turn one's attention the other way, to switch and refresh one's emotional condition. *Yijung-Byunqi* therapy is one of the main methods used in traditional Korean medical practice today to prevent or treat mind-related illnesses. Activities such as music, painting, dances, calligraphy, I-go, fishing or travelling have been used for *Yijung-Byunqi*. It can also be achieved through empathetic dialogue. *Yijung-Byunqi* therapy has been applied to depression, impulse control disorders, anxiety disorders and stress neurosis in the TKM psychiatry. Supportive, suggestive or ventilation psychotherapy may be close to this method.

Gyungja-Pyungji *therapy* 경자평지 요법

This involves desensitising unease or anxiety. *Gyungja-Pyungji* literally meaning 'startled person, to ease' is to alleviate the intensity of the stimulus by gradually raising it, until one ceases to be anxious. *Gyungja-Pyungji* therapy (驚者平之療法), first mentioned by Chinese physician Jang Ja-Hwa in the twelfth century, has a methodological similarity to flooding or systematic desensitisation sometimes called extended exposure therapy, a type of behavioural therapy used to help remove phobia and other anxiety disorders. It also includes factors of the didactic technique of cognitive behavioural therapy.

Ohji-Sangseung *therapy* 오지상승 요법

Based on the theory of the interrelationships of the five elements (earth, water, fire, metal and wood), it is to treat illness by applying the sequential subjugations of the five emotions. *Ohji-Sangseung* found in Hwangei-Naekyung literally means 'be aware of the five elements, beat one another'. Using the emotion in counterpart to the initial emotion experienced by the patient, enables the patient to regain their stability. According to the principle the five elements, earth, water, fire, metal and wood respectively correspond to anxiety, fear, joy, sorrow and anger. Earth (anxiety) beats water (fear); water beats fire (joy); fire beats metal (sorrow); metal beats wood (anger); wood beats earth (anxiety). Today, *Ohji-Sangseung* therapy (五志相勝療法) is generally applied in TKM psychiatry proving that many mental illnesses such as panic, depression, somatoform disorders and some symptoms of schizophrenia have been improved by *Ohji-Sangseung* therapy.

Traditional Korean medicine

During the period of the Three Kingdoms (57BC–AD668), Chinese and Indian medicines were adopted, forming the foundation to traditional Korean medicine. Korean medicine flourished in the Joseon Period (1392–1897) and many books on Korean medicine were published. In traditional oriental medicine, illness was understood as a result of disharmony in nature and disharmony among the internal organs, thus treatment was to make the organs harmonious with nature. This Taoist view was the basic theory of Korean medicine before the *Sasang-Uihak*. The medicine and medical theorists at the time considered a human as a part of nature and placed great importance on the harmony and correspondence between humanity and nature.[4] *Dongui-Bogam* was written under this influence by Heo Jun. On the other hand, Lee Jei-Ma whose philosophy was weighted more to Neo-Confucianism, thought that human beings exist independently of nature and mind had the same importance as body. He appreciated the role of mind in the formation of the constitution and mental stabilisation by striking a balance between body and mind as the curative method. He systematised his thoughts into the *Sasang-Uihak*.

Generally, traditional Korean medicine emphasised specific characteristics of the individuals instead of single symptoms. It took the view that a disease sprang from thoughts or feelings. The most distinct feature of TKM differing from traditional Chinese medicine was this human and mind-centred approach. Hence, TKM's ultimate objective was to prevent diseases by controlling mind and nurturing it in daily life. This was elaborated both in *Dongui-Bogam* and with the *Sasang-Uihak*. To control one's mind, one had to cultivate '*Tao* 도 (道)' according to *Dongui-Bogam* and 'righteous mind' according to the *Sasang-Uihak*.

Dongui-Bogam 동의 보감

Dongui-Bogam (東醫 寶鑑; Treasured Mirror of Eastern Medicine),[5] described as an encyclopaedia of traditional East Asian medical practices, was edited and published in twenty-five volumes, each of twenty-five chapters, by the Joseon era court physician Heo Jun 허 준 (1539–1615) in 1613. He included everything about Eastern medicine but also absorbed and digested all the contents of traditional Korean medicine and reorganised them creating a new paradigm of TKM in *Dongui-Bogam*. Heo Jun initially worked for the royals and aristocrats, while putting greater effort into producing treatments that were accessible to the commoners. *Dongui-Bogam* described every herbal medicine indigenous to Korea. He travelled all over the place and crisscrossed the mountains to find all herb remedies, i.e., '*Hyangyakk* 향약 (鄕藥; Korean wild herbs which were grown in the countryside)', which ordinary people could easily find and obtain on the Korean Peninsula. After he had assembled them all, studied and classified each herb, he presented those herbs to people with the names indicated in *Hangeul* 한글 (Korean letters) in place of *Hanja* 漢字 (Chinese characters) which most ordinary people of the time did not read. With *Dongui-Bogam*, traditional Korean medicine achieved its status distinct from traditional Chinese medicine. Instead of handling diseases one by one, *Dongui-Bogam* took as its medical stance that each patient should be treated from a holistic point of view based on the idea that human beings could not live without nature and everything in nature had an effect on human beings. It classified each person according to both external and internal characteristics and provided customised cures, which inspired traditional Korean medicine to become fundamentally human-centred medicine.

The concepts found in *Dongui-Bogam* originated from *Seondo*, a traditional Korean way of living which advocated accumulating *Jung*, *Gi* and *Shin*: *Jung* 정 (精) as body essence and sexual energy; *Gi* 기 (氣) as life-force energy and breath; *Shin* 신 (神) as spirit and foundation of *Jung* and *Gi*. In modern science, *Jung* is matter; *Shin* is consciousness; *Gi* is subtle energy as passageway between *Jung* and *Shin*. Health meant the smooth circulation of these elements that are, in

Figure 3.5 Heo Jun

Figure 3.6 Dongui-Bogam

the view of *Tao*, the most important factors in humans. Heo Jun thought that basically all the diseases were a result of erroneous care of *Jung*, *Gi* and *Shin*. *Dongui-Bogam* referred to *Yangsaeng-Sul* 양생술 (養生術; The Life-Nurturing Treatment) that was to live candidly through soundly nurturing *Jung*, *Gi* and *Shin*.

Dongui-Bogam, in its Naekyung Volume One, illustrated the examples of mental illness, extracted from the Chinese medicine books. Those mentioned in the book were akin to depressive-manic syndrome (*Jeon-Kwang*), dissociative disorder (*Sasu*), hysteria (*Jang-Jo*), panic disorder (*Sim-Damdam-Daedong*), post-traumatic stress disorder (*Talyoung-Siljung*) and anger illness (*Ganwul-Hwahwa*). *Dongui-Bogam* presented *Heoshim-Hapdo* 허심합도 (虛心合道) and *Yido* therapy 이도요법 (以道療法) as treatment methods. *Heoshim-Hapdo* refers to the 'Cultivation of Mind' and *Yido* therapy means 'Therapy through *Tao* 도 (道)'. It noted that to cure a disease, one must treat a patient's mind first. It claimed that if mind was pure, illness would cure itself without medicine. According to *Dongui-Bogam*, what caused an illness of mind were mainly greed, fear and repressed anger. Before administering medicine and acupuncture treatment, it was, thus, essential to set aside one's greed, fear and repressed anger as well as cultivating the mind along with having a proper diet and a good lifestyle. It equally underlined the importance of personal maturation and the practice of *Tao*, engendering an empathetic, positive and active attitude, and trust in the treatment as an indispensable component of mind in the process of treatment. *Dongui-Bogam* written in the early seventeenth century is highly esteemed even today and still remains as a valuable reference in the practice of TKM, especially its concepts which focus on prevention before developing a disease and emphasis on a healthy mind in treating disease.

Sasang-Uihak 사상의학

The *Sasang-Uihak* (四象醫學; Four Constitutions Medicine) was a traditional Korean medical typology, which was methodically theorised and organised by a scholar Lee Jei-Ma 이제마 (1837–1900) in his book '*Dongui-Susae-Bowon* 동의수세보원 (The Principle of Life Preservation in Oriental Medicine)'. Lee Jei-Ma travelled all over the country and to foreign countries to study and train himself before he established his own thought and developed a theory that sharply differed from traditional oriental medicine. He laid out in his book in 1894 that medication and nursing should be individualised according to one's *Sasang* 사상 (四象; four constitutions) type.

The *Sasang-Uihak* was based on the Neo-Confucian views of nature and humanity. Lee Jei-Ma, who was a follower of the Realist School or *Silhak* 실학 (實學) of Neo-Confucianism, was particularly influenced by his teacher Dasan Jeong Yak-Yong 정약용 (1762–1836) who viewed nature as constant change, advocated the independence and individuality of human beings and stressed the importance of creating a harmony in their interactions. The *Sasang-Uihak* emerged from a view of the human as an independent existence, and that the health of the human body had a close relationship with the states of mind. Human mind and body were not separate and they closely reflected each other, and the aspect of mind needed to be considered when examining causes of a disease. Thus, not only food and the natural environment but also emotional changes in

Figure 3.7 Lee Jei-Ma

humans could be another major reason for illness. The *Sasang-Uihak*'s most distinctive feature was the idea that medical diagnosis and treatment should be based on a person's typology rather than on symptoms, and each person should be given different prescriptions depending on the constitution of the individual.

The theoretical rationale of *Sasang* typology derived from Chinese *Sasang* theory which explained the composition and movements of the universe through the fundamental rule of relativity of '*Yin-Yang*' and '*Sasang* (a four-axis schema)'. Under this theory, the human body was classified into four constitutions of *Tae-Yang* (greater *Yang*), *So-Yang* (lesser *Yang*), *Tae-Yin* (greater *Yin*), *So-Yin* (lesser *Yin*) according to the weakness or excess of *Yin* and *Yang* and the individual's temperament and nature. These four constitutional types stemmed from variations in the four physical and four mental differentiations. The four physical organ systems referred to lung, spleen, liver and kidney. The four mental notions were sorrow, anger, joy and pleasure, which were defined as '*Seong-Jeong* 성정 (性情; innate nature-emotional disposition)'. *Sasang* theory explained human beings as an ongoing display of the four constitutions differentiated by the lesser or greater organ structure scheme formed through the manifestation of *Seong-Jeong*.

The main philosophical basis of *Sasang* theory was its emphasis on the importance of humans and interpersonal relationships. Humans existed independently of nature and were influenced by two factors, namely social environment and human affairs. Based on this philosophy, Lee Jei-Ma interpreted a holistic medicine which embraced the physical, mental and social wellness of an individual within the completely human-centred paradigm. In *Sasang* typology, the main cause of disease lay in an imbalance between the functional strengths of the organ structures, which arose from the imbalance of the rising and descending *Gi* (life-force energy) of *Seong* 성 (性; innate nature) and *Jeong* 정 (情; emotional disposition). Control and containment of the *Seong-Jeong* was one of the unique foundational medical philosophies of *Sasang-Uihak*. The primary goal of treatment was, thus, to learn to manage one's *Seong-Jeong* through righteous mind by advocating lifestyles compatible with a given constitutional makeup. Mencius' philosophy of 'rectification of the self through controlling the mind' led to the *Sasang* therapeutic approach of 'controlling the mind to heal the body'. According to the *Sasang-Uihak*, one could control one's illness when one returned to and retained the state of a 'righteous mind'. The principle of *Joong-Yong* 중용 (中庸; The Doctrine of the Mean) to maintain balance and harmony by directing the mind to a state of constant equilibrium was clearly pivotal in the *Sasang-Uihak*.

Based on *Sasang* theory and Neo-Confucianism, the *Sasang-Uihak*, however, did not just rely on the existing theory of *Yin-Yang* and the Five Elements (五行). Instead, it focused on the constitution of each individual in the process of treatment. The *Sasang-Uihak* explained the constitutionally unique attributes that controlled the functional balance of physiology and pathology. In *Sasang* typology, differentiated therapeutics applied to different constitutional types, or different medicines applied to the same disease were enacted according to an individual's constitutional type, personality and psychological status, as well as nutritional state, functioning of internal organs, medical reaction and environmental factors. It was fundamentally a tailored treatment which embraced specific constitutional medication, diet, physical training and psychological caution within the context of an individual. Physical, environmental or psychological causes of illness do not evenly affect all individuals. Different individuals each with a different constitutional disposition display different degrees of weakness and sensitiveness. The *Sasang-Uihak* explained individual differences in patterns of physical feature, behavioural tendency, psychological traits and susceptibility to a certain illness. In this regard, the *Sasang-Uihak* was a traditional Korean medicine based on personality. Furthermore, the *Sasang-Uihak* had a view that the resolution of personal or social conflicts was mostly dependent on the development of self-cultivation that the distressed individual exercises through interaction with others, and remedies the self. This process of self-cultivation would regulate the mind, resulting in the acquisition of balance between mind and body, between human and nature, and thus the cure.

Grounded on the treatment that was to regulate the mind and restore the original constitutional balance to manage the illness, the *Sasang-Uihak* was essentially a mind-centred approach. It was based on one's ability to manage oneself through lifestyle and behaviour changes compatible with a given constitutional makeup, whereby one would also prevent potential weaknesses and illnesses and preserve health and longevity. In this sense, the *Sasang-Uihak* was also preventive medicine. Today, the *Sasang-Uihak* is widely used by the traditional Korean medicine doctors in the clinical diagnosis and treatment of disease. A number of TKM doctors have been successfully applying its theory and thoughts to clinical practice.

Notes

1 The TKM professionals acquired their national recognition in 2002 and oriental psychiatric specialists obtained their first certification in 2003. Approximately twenty oriental psychiatric specialists are being certified every year. Since August 2005, oriental psychiatric treatments in Korea (inclusive of the methods presented in the text) are covered by the National Health Insurance.

2 *Samguk-Sagi* is a historical record of the Three Kingdoms of Korea: Goguryeo (37BC–AD668), Baekje (18BC–AD660), and Silla (57BC–AD935). It was undertaken by the government official and historian Kim Bu-Sik 김부식 and a team of junior scholars and completed in 1145 during the Goryeo Dynasty (918–1392).

3 *Samguk-Yusa* is a collection of legends, folktales and historical accounts relating to the Three Kingdoms of Korea. It was complied by the Buddhist monk Iryeon 일연 (1206–1289).

4 Medical theorists at that time tried to explain medical theory and causes of sickness by *Yin-Yang* and the Five Phase Theory: The Five Phases are Earth (Stomach/Spleen), Metal (Lung, Large Intestine), Wood (Liver/Gallbladder), Fire (Heart/Small Intestine) and Water (Kidney/Bladder). Each of these phases has specific characteristics attributed to it, and these characteristics are concentrated within the mind and body of the individual who belongs to that phase.

5 The compilation of the books began during Korea's Joseon era after the seven-year struggle against Japanese invasion at the turn of the sixteenth century. Famine and disease soon followed, providing impetus for the compilation of the books. The King commanded him to publish the medical book that puts Eastern medicine together. In 2009, the UNESCO appointed this book to 'Memory of the World' for its spirit of the times, originality, importance in world history.

Bibliography

Chae, H. et al. (2003). An Alternative Way to Individualized Medicine: Psychological and Physical Traits of Sasang Typology. *Journal of Alternative and Complementary Medicine*, 9 (4), 519–528.

Choi, S. H. (1996). *Dongui.Susae.Bowon (the principle of life preservation in oriental medicine)*. Seoul: Kyunghee University Press. [Korean]

Kim, K. I. (1972). Psychoanalytic consideration of Korean Shamanism. *Journal of the Korean Neuropsychiatric Association*, 11 (2), 121–129. [Korean]

Ko, M. S. (2011). *Looking for the Vision on Body, Cosmos, and Life*. Seoul: Greenbee. [Korean]

Kwan, B. H. (2001). A study of Gyungj.Pyungji treatment and behaviour and cognitive therapy. *Journal of Oriental Neuropsychiatry*, 12 (1), 47–57 [Korean]

Lee, E. J., & Song, I. B. (1999). The study of Lee Jei-Ma's Sasang philosophy. *Journal of Sasang Constitutional Medicine*, 11 (1), 15–23. [Korean]

Lee, H. J. (1997). Study on the contrasting aspects between Sasang constitutional medicine and traditional oriental medicine. *Journal of Sasang Constitutional Medicine*, 9 (2), 95–145. [Korean]

Lee, S. K. (2000). Cognitive therapy and Oriental Psychotherapy. *Journal of Oriental Neuropsychiatry*, 11 (2), 169–175. [Korean]

Rhi, B.Y. (1999). Psychotherapy in Eastern tradition. *Shimsung.Yeonku*, 14 (1), 14–28. [Korean]

Rhi, B.Y., & Seo, K. R.(1994). Psychotherapeutic implication of the Korean shamanistic healing ceremony, *Shimsung.Yeonku*, 9 (1&2), 43–135. [Korean]

Song, I. B. (1996). Lee Jei-Ma's views on sciences and philosophy. *Journal of Sasang Constitutional Medicine*, 8 (2), 1–10. [Korean]

4 First psychiatry

Modern psychiatry was first introduced to Korea largely by two streams during the colonial period (1910–1945). The first was through the missionary institutions that were based on the humanistic approach in the spirit of Christianity, and worked towards providing Korean people with medical services and educational training. The second was through colonial governmental institutions that were primarily built for the Japanese residents in Korea, and placed strict restrictions on access to them by Korean people. During this period, Japanese psychiatry was heavily influenced by Kraepelinian descriptive psychiatry from Germany, being what was mostly taught and practised in Korea. Consequently, confinement was the most common treatment performed around this period, followed by occupational therapy, sleep therapy, fever therapy, insulin shock therapy and electroconvulsive therapy (ECT). In the early part of twentieth century, albeit in a very scattered, episodic manner, Freudian psychoanalysis was also introduced.

After the Liberation (1945), in spite of political and social tensions, Korea's modern psychiatry gradually progressed, especially during the Korean War (1950–1953), when training and development of facilities were expanded with support from the UN Medical Group which organised a mental hygiene programme. The graduates from this programme had an opportunity to go abroad and upon their return they changed and developed Korean psychiatry under the influence of American dynamic psychiatry. While they contributed to increasing the number of private psychiatric institutions, in the 1960s more people were beginning to use psychiatric clinics and hospitals. However, mental health professionals and training facilities were still few and the understanding of the general public about mental health was very poor.

Introduction of Western psychiatry

Jejung-won 제중원 *(1885–1904)*

Western knowledge about science and medicine was introduced into Korea in the mid-seventeenth century by Korean Confucian and Taoist scholars who had developed a great interest in Western ideas through the Chinese translations of the books. Nonetheless, it mostly remained as a personal interest on acquiring the knowledge from reading books and medical knowledge was not put into practice. However, by the late nineteenth century, modern Western medicine introduced by both Western missionaries and Japanese military physicians began to be used in practice. The knowledge of modern psychiatry itself was introduced into Korea around the same period.

When a prominent political figure and nephew of Empress Min, Min Young-Ik was gravely injured by assailants one night in December 1884, Horace N. Allen (1858–1932), an American Northern Presbyterian missionary who entered Korea in 1884 as a doctor-attaché of the American embassy, was asked in the emergency to treat the critically injured Min Young-Ik. By disinfecting the wounds, staunching severed arteries and suturing deeply cut wounds, Allen saved his life. The success of the treatment impressed King Gojong 고종 and those who had witnessed the operation. In January 1885, Allen asked King Gojong to build a small hospital to treat Koreans and foster Korean doctors for practising Western medicine in Korea. The same year in April, Jejung-won 제중원 (濟衆院; House of Universal Helpfulness, 1885–1904),[1] the first Western hospital was opened. In the following year, sixteen Koreans were accepted as medical students and received the very first training in Western medicine in Korean history.

Jejung-won presented an outstanding contrast to the later-established Japanese government hospital with its prime purpose of treating Korean people and more importantly instructing Korean medical students in the ideals of Western medicine. After having worked for a year with his colleague Heron, Allen wrote an annual report to the missionary board in America. In this first year's report on Jejung-won (4.10.1885–4.10.1886), Allen provided detailed data on the patients he had treated. It contained invaluable information concerning the disease patterns of the time, according great significance to the history of modern medicine in Korea. In this report, Allen and Heron divided diseases largely into 18 categories

Figure 4.1 Jejung-won, 1885–1904

and gave the first classification of mental diseases of Korean patients. The statistics showed a relatively high rate of hysterical patients (33 cases). In 'Category V: Diseases of the Nervous System', 12 cases of delirium tremens, 13 cases of insanity (6 mania, 5 melancholy and 3 Dementia), 1 case of nervous prostration and 3 cases of insomnia were listed. Additionally, it reported 2 cases of anorexia under 'Category II: Diseases of the Digestive System'. How these patients were treated, however, was not discussed in the report.

In 1893, the Church appointed Oliver R. Avison (1860–1956), a missionary doctor from Toronto, Canada to run Jejung-won. Under his direction, Jejung-won Medical School was officially recognised in 1899 by the government as a private teaching institute and the medical education began to take more systematic shape. In spite of many difficulties, Avison prepared and published medical textbooks in Korean on various subjects of basic medical sciences such as hygiene, physiology and anatomy. Unfortunately, these textbooks were banned from use when Japan took over the rule of Korean government in 1910. In 1899, while on leave in North America, Avison was invited to speak at a conference of missionaries in New York where he elaborated on the medical project in Korea. Louis H. Severance, a businessperson and philanthropist from Cleveland, Ohio, was in attendance and deeply moved. Severance paid for the major portion of the construction costs of new buildings for the medical facility in Korea. In April 1904, the Presbyterian mission in Korea renamed the reconstructed Jejung-won and the medical education institution as the 'Severance Hospital and Medical School'. In 1908, the first seven graduates from the Severance received their doctors' licences from the Korean government. Nevertheless, the Severance Hospital did not have a psychiatric department until Charles I. McLaren, an Australian missionary psychiatrist, joined the Severance as a lecturer.

Charles I. McLaren / The Severance 세브란스 (1913–1938)

In 1911, Charles I. McLaren 마나연 (馬羅連, 1882–1957), an Australian psychiatrist, came to work at Paton memorial hospital in Jinju 진주 배돈병원 as a medical missionary. From 1913, McLaren taught neurology and psychological medicine at the Severance Union Medical College[2] until 1939, when the rejection of demands from the Japanese government for Shinto worship led to his resignation. In 1923, he established the Department of Psychiatry at the Severance Hospital where he practised his psychiatric examinations and treatments. In 1930, he realised his long-cherished ambition of building a psychiatric ward. It could accommodate only three male and three female patients but was decorated with great care with a garden so that patients staying there could feel safe and relaxed. McLaren believed that mental illness could be treated simply by restoring meaning or goal in life. His humanistic view with its sensitivity to human rights of the mentally ill was completely in contrast to the biological approach of Japanese colonial psychiatry. The Japanese colonial government was not supportive of his humanistic approach in favour of Koreans.

As a faithful Christian and compassionate and dynamic man, McLaren dedicated himself to the humanitarian care of people who were mentally ill and always stood on the patients' side advocating their rights and fighting prejudice against the mentally ill. He played a decisive role in implementing this humanitarian approach towards patients at the Department of Psychiatry of Severance Medical College. According to his 'disciples', he sometimes spent two or three hours with one patient. He was also an advocate for the right for patients to return to their previous activities upon recovery. He claimed that someone who has suffered from mental illness can recover from it like any physical illness, and thus has the right to regain their former function in society upon recovery. Under his influence, several medical students pursued psychiatry as a major filed of study. Among them was Lee Jung-Chul, the first Korean doctor formally trained in psychiatry who later became the first Korean career psychiatrist.

However, Charles I. McLaren's humanistic approach did not survive because the Japanese colonial government forced him to resign in 1939, closely followed by the premature death of his successor, Lee Jung-Chul in 1945 at the age of 41. Thankfully, some of his students carried on specialising in psychiatry during the difficult period of the early 1940s. They made a major contribution to the growth of modern psychiatry in Korea after the Liberation. After his forced resignation, Charles I. McLaren returned to the Jinju Hospital, but was arrested immediately after the bombing of Pearl Harbor and imprisoned for eleven weeks before repatriation to Australia in November 1942. However, he continued affectionate

Figure 4.2 The Severance Hospital and Medical School; students and staff at the Severance, 1904

communication with the Severance Union Medical College until 1957 when he passed away.

Joseon-Chongdokbu Uiwon / Kyungseong imperial university hospital

The Japanese Residency-General was set up in Korea in 1905, and in practice the colonial government started before the Japanese annexation of Korea in 1910. By integrating or abolishing the existing medical institutions and schools, they established Daehan Uiwon 대한의원 in 1907. It was officially a Korean governmental hospital but in reality it was only as an instrument of Japanese colonialism. As the colonial government took control of everything in 1910, Daehan Uiwon was reorganised to 'Joseon-Chongdokbu Uiwon 조선총독부 의원 (Hospital of the Japanese Government-General of Korea, 1910–1928)', which was composed mainly of Japanese doctors and officers with a very limited number of Koreans.

To administrate for the mentally ill patients, it arranged two different facilities. One was 'Jesaeng-won' that featured detention. The other was 'Ward 8' that highlighted the treatment element. 'Jesaeng-won 제생원 (濟生院; health care centre for commoners)', was established in 1911 for fostering orphans, educating the blind and caring for the mentally ill. Between March and September 1912, the number of mental patients was around 86 and it was probably the first large-scale residential facility for the mentally ill in Korea. However, it was strongly characterised by its function as a place for confinement and isolation. According to the second annual report of Joseon-Chongdokbu Uiwon (1912–1913), those hospitalised mental patients were mainly those who had been brought in by the police because of diverse behavioural problems that they caused in local communities. The descriptions of the behaviour problems included habitual stealing, violent fighting, fraud, ward wandering, threatening behaviour, arson, sexual deviants and those with a homicidal tendency. Obviously, these descriptions did not directly infer a mental illness and they were simply under observation while being hospitalised. The inpatients referred from other departments of the hospital were those who manifested some psychiatric complications of physical diseases, for example, dementia praecox or central nervous system syphilis. In 1913, Joseon-Chongdokbu Uiwon took over the function of Jesaeng-won for care of the mental patients.

Before 1913, the Department of Internal Medicine of Joseon-Chongdokbu Uiwon treated the mentally ill patients. In 1911 only, 1,276 patients received treatment and 1,223 cases were treated for neurasthenia. Nevertheless, the hospital at this time functioned as a facility exclusively for Japanese residents in Korea, with very limited access available to local Koreans except a few privileged and rich Koreans. Only 193 patients were Koreans among the number of 1,223 and except in 3 cases, they were all treated for neurasthenia. In 1913, the Department of Psychiatry (until 1921, it was called 'the Department of Mental Disease') branched off from the Department of Internal Medicine and became independent with an inpatient ward of 20 rooms and 35 beds. The treatment modalities practised in the hospital and carried out by Japanese professional staff ranged from occupational therapy, outdoor therapy, hypnotherapy to hot bath therapy. Between 1911 and 1916, Shim Ho-Seob was the first and only Korean at the Department. In April 1928, a newly built psychiatric ward was inaugurated with 480 beds.

Joseon-Chongdokbu Uiwon and its psychiatric unit became an affiliated teaching hospital of the Medical College of Kyungseong (Keisei) Imperial University 경성제국대학 의학부 부속의원 (1928–1945) in May 1928. Consequently, psychiatry in Korea experienced a transition from focusing on treatment to becoming more focused on education and research. The Kyungseong Imperial University was strictly a Japanese university that was open only to Japanese nationals. It was many years later that a few privileged and outstanding Korean students were admitted as exceptions. In over 35 years of Japanese colonisation of Korea, there were only six or seven Korean psychiatrists trained at this university. Due to discrimination against Korean graduates for faculty positions at the Medical College, trained Korean psychiatrists during this period opened private practices or changed to internal medicine, resulting in hindrance to the development of Korean modern psychiatry in subsequent years. The Medical College of Kyungseong Imperial University developed into the Seoul National University (SNU) Medical School in 1946 and Shim Ho-Seob was appointed as its first dean and Myung Ju-Wan as the first director of SNU Hospital.

First Korean psychiatrists

Lee Jung-Chul was considered to be the first legitimate Korean psychiatrist who evinced a clear distinction between psychiatry and internal medicine. Before him, there was Shim Ho-Seob who had worked with mentally ill people and taught neurology in the early 1910s but he switched to internal medicine. At the Severance Union Medical College in which the Department of Psychiatry branched off from that of Internal Medicine in 1923, there were six Koreans who worked as assistant professors between 1914 and 1925. Among them were Lee Su-Won and Kim Tak-Won. Lee Su-Won 이수원 was the first graduate from the Severance Medical College (1919), who specialised in psychiatry and worked under McLaren until 1928. He published an article 'The Simon-Binet Intelligence Test Method' in the *Severance Bulletin* (1926, 8: 32–33), but no further reported academic research activities have been found since then. The *Severance Bulletin* reported that he opened a private clinic but none of his medical activities was recorded thereafter. A photo of him teaching students appeared in the album of graduates in 1935, so it is possible that he may have continued to work as a part-time lecturer at the Severance for several more years, or taught there in 1934–1935 when Lee Jung-Chul went to Japan for his doctoral study. Kim Tak-Won 김탁원 who studied at the Kyungseong Medical College and graduated in 1921, received further training in psychiatry in Japan. However, he became more involved in social and political activities than in psychiatry, although he continued to practise in his private clinic. Clearly, the small number of Korean psychiatrists before 1945 was mainly because of severe discrimination against Koreans in their academic careers, and hence the extremely limited number of psychiatry teaching staff in Korea. Also, the activities of the first generation of Korean psychiatrists are scarce or unrecorded.

Lee Jung-Chul 이중철

Lee Jung-Chul (1904–1945) was the first career psychiatrist, first Korean professor at the Department of Psychiatry, and first Korean doctorate majoring in psychiatry. In 1924, he entered the Severance Medical College. After graduation in 1927, he worked as a general practitioner. In 1929, he went back to the Severance as an assistant professor in the Department of Psychiatry and carried out research at the Kyungseong Imperial University (June to December 1929) at the same time. In the 1930s, he conducted and published several pieces of research, mainly focused on the biological aspects of mental disorders.

Encouraged by his teacher, McLaren, who was always his keen supporter, Lee Jung-Chul went abroad to acquire further training and experience. In October 1931, he went to the Peking Union Medical College in China to conduct research for six months. One year after his return to the Severance from China, he left for the Kyushu University Japan to pursue a doctoral study. In 1935, he became the first doctorate in psychiatry from Korea. He published his thesis 'The Origin of Senile Plaques' in an American medical journal *Archives of Neurology and Psychiatry* (1936, 18). While he was still studying in Japan, Lee Jung-Chul travelled to Australia. After visiting 'Callan Park Hospital (1878–1914)', a psychiatric hospital in a suburb of Sydney, he was deeply impressed by the governmental support and system adopted by Australia in caring for mentally ill patients. In 1937, Lee Jung-Chul became the dean of the Psychiatric Department of the Severance Medical College. However, after being involved in some in-school matters,[3] he resigned just before McLaren resigned in 1938, and started private practice. His activities during the period of private practice were not much known.

Lee Jung-Chul has great significance as the first mental health professional who as early as 1935, considered mental illness as the most critical health issue along with tuberculosis and leprosy. While McLaren took the humanistic approach to psychiatry, Lee Jung-Chul put more stress on the scientific aspect of psychiatry. Unfortunately, he died prematurely at the age of 41 in April 1945 during the epidemic of typhus fever, preventing him from further contribution to the development of modern Korean psychiatry. Kim Joong-Ryoul 김중률 graduating in 1933 from the Severance Union Medical College, who took over the Psychiatric Department while Lee Jung-Chul was away to study, remembered him as a very kind, dedicated doctor who willingly helped the poor people.

Shim Ho-Seob 심호섭

Shim Ho-Seob (1890–1973) was the first Korean who was trained and practised in psychiatry under the Japanese colonial government. He was impressed by the speedy recovery of a sick relative in the Severance Hospital and decided to be a medical doctor. In 1909, he entered the Daehan Uiwon Medical College. Working in Jesaeng-won, he had close contact with the mentally ill people and had extensive clinical experience. He served at Joseon-Chongdokbu Uiwon and the Kyungseong Medical College between 1911 and 1916 as the only appointed Korean doctor; the Japanese institutions operating gross discrimination against Korean professionals required simply a doctor who could communicate in Korean. In 1917, Shim Ho-Seob moved to the Severance to teach neurology in the Department of Internal Medicine and changed his career to an internal medicine doctor. From 1922 to 1925, he studied at the University of Tokyo and received a doctoral degree in 1926. Then, he returned to the Severance. Later, he participated in the establishment of the Korean Neuropsychiatric Association (1945) and presided over it for five terms until 1950 when Myung Ju-Wan took over the presidency.

Myung Ju-Wan 명주완

Myung Ju-Wan (1905–1977) pioneered the education of neuropsychiatry in Korea and took the lead in the settlement of Korean psychiatry. He studied at the Kyungseong Medical College (1924–1930). Upon his graduation, he worked in the Department of Pharmacology doing research until 1934, and then moved to the Neuropsychiatry Department. Around 1935, he first introduced a German medical scientist's (Sakel) insulin coma treatment into clinical practice. In 1938, he obtained a doctorate in pharmacology at the Kyoto Imperial University Japan. Around the same time, he opened the Seongbuk Hospital with two other associates and started to treat mentally ill people. However, details of their clinical practices is unrecorded. After the Liberation, he was appointed as the director of the Seoul National University (SNU) Hospital and contributed to establishing the Korean Neuropsychiatric Association over which he presided from 1951 to 1961. Myung Ju-Wan was deemed to be an excellent administrator, as well as an enthusiastic practitioner and educator, who successfully promoted the advocacy of medical rights and the formulation of an ethical health care policy at the beginning of Korean psychiatry.

Reconstruction of Korean psychiatry

After the Liberation in 1945, the 'Korean Neuropsychiatric Association' was immediately organised and academic meetings were held regularly at the Department of Psychiatry of Kyungseong Imperial University, now known as the Seoul National University. During this period, the population of patients with general paresis and addiction by narcotics prevailed, as well as those with major psychotic and neurological disorders. Around this time, the private institutions such as Seongbuk Hospital (run by Myung Ju-Wan, 1938) and Chungryangri-Nwoe Hospital (run by Choi Shin-Hae, 1945, the later Chungryangri Mental Hospital 청량리정신병원) provided the care and treatment for the mentally ill.

Chungryangri-Nwoe Hospital was the first hospital that specialised in psychiatry, having 280 beds. At the beginning, the patients who received the treatment were mostly the mentally ill with syphilis. After the war, the hospital had more patients with neurosis, schizophrenia and depression.

Between 1945 and 1950, in spite of the political tension in the Korean Peninsula due to the ideological conflicts between the 'left' and the 'right', dividing Korea into two entirely different regions, new municipal and provincial mental hospitals were established: Kyungkido Hospital 경기도 도립병원 (1945); Sounhwa Hospital 순화시립병원 (drug-addicts clinic, 1947). In 1946, the Psychiatric Department at Seoul Woman's Medical College 서울여자의과대학 was founded. In 1947 and 1950, child psychiatrists and clinical psychologists came from the United States as lecturers or exchange professors extending educational programmes. However, psychiatric services fell behind their with the need for them. *Dong-A* daily newspaper 동아일보 reported in 1949 on the state of mental health provision, describing the absence of government policies on mental health and the urgent need for psychiatric services. At that stage, there were only nine psychiatry specialists for a total of 200,000 mentally ill patients.

The deployment of American military forces from 1945 and the Korean War (1950–1953) gave, albeit with a tragic outcome, Korean psychiatrists the opportunity to have contact with American military psychiatrists and American psychiatric literature. During the war, all available psychiatrists had been confined to Army duty. American military psychiatrists stimulated these Korean psychiatrists and psychiatry candidates with new forms of trainings and encouraged them to pursue further training. Although many psychiatrists disappeared and the public mental hospitals stopped their operations during the Korean War, Korean psychiatry rapidly restored its status after the war and began its radical change and development with a new training system. Under the dominating influences of American dynamic psychiatry in the 1950s, the teaching of Kraepelinian descriptive psychiatry was replaced by the American dynamic psychiatry of Adolf Meyer. Since 1958, intern and residency training programmes have been adopted. The Korean Neuropsychiatric Association took over the board examination for neuropsychiatry specialists. Pedo-psychiatry and mental hygiene, especially relating to child problems, began to progress.

A few more hospitals were established during these years, including the Neuropsychiatry Department of Chonnam University Medical School (1952), Busan Youngrak Sanatorium 부산 영락정신 요양원 (1953), National Noryangjin Mental Hospital 국립 노량진 정신구호 병원 (1954) and National Mental Institution 국립 정신질환자 수용소 (1956, later the National Naju Mental Hospital 국립 나주 병원) in addition to some military hospitals. During this period, the cases of schizophrenia treated by hospitals accounted for more than half of the total number of patients with mental illness. Seventy per cent of patients were in their twenties and thirties. Insulin coma therapy and fever therapy with typhoid vaccine were still used along with ECT (electro-convulsive therapy) and pharmacotherapy. New methods of psychiatric treatment such as chlorpromazine were also introduced.[4]

The progress of Korean psychiatry faltered a little when a military coup d'état[5] took place in 1961. Although there were five psychiatric departments in medical schools and about thirteen private psychiatric clinics and hospitals, most of them were inadequate in their set-ups and the facilities were very limited in meeting the national needs. More seriously, the lack of a wider experience of psychiatrists in the field of mental health and insufficient understanding of the methods for treatment became problematic. In addition, it was still very common to find that the treatment of much mental illness was tried first with superstitious devices or folk medications such as plant poison.[6] Only after a long delay, usually when the illness had become chronic or the patient became paralysed as a result of this medication, would they consult a medical doctor who then might refer them to a psychiatrist. Furthermore, mentally ill patients were apt to be judged in terms of failure, sin, cowardice or perversity. Particularly from the 1960s through the 1970s until the early 1980s, the social defence policies of the military government were prominent and a confinement-oriented policy was carried out under the premise that 'the mentally ill are dangerous'.

On the other hand, many American-trained psychiatrists who began returning from 1957 onwards held more positions in medical schools and set up more private clinics. They taught dynamic psychiatry and psychotherapy. Theories of Freudian psychoanalysis and Neo-Freudian schools, psychosomatic medicine, preventive psychiatry and concerns of child guidance were also introduced by psychiatrists inspired by American dynamic psychiatry. The first National Mental Hospital 국립 정신병원 (now known as Seoul National Hospital 국립 서울병원) was inaugurated in 1962 under the motto of the World Health Organisation (WHO), offering 360 beds, and collaborations with the Ministry of Health and Social Affairs for Korean mental heath movement began to increase. Among the psychiatrists who were very active during this reconstructing period of Korean psychiatry, there were notably Kim Sung-Hi, Rhee Dong-Shick and Yu Seok-Jin.

Kim Sung-Hi 김성희

Kim Sung-Hi (1917–2003) is considered to be the first Korean psychoanalyst and also the first mental health professional to apply the approach that was person-centred before the term 'Person-Centered Counselling' of Carl Rogers was introduced to Korea in 1962. He had his initial medical training at the Pyongyang Medical University 평양의전. Impressed by Freud's book *Interpretation of Dreams*, he decided to go to Japan to study psychoanalysis. He arrived in Japan in April 1940 and studied psychoanalysis at the Sendai Imperial University until January 1945. After the Liberation, he worked at the Seoul National University Medical School for one year. Then, he moved to the Psychiatric Department of Pyongyang Medical University Hospital and worked there for about four years from August 1946. During this time, he was tortured for practising psychoanalysis under the communist regime of North Korea which rejected any forms of mind-related activity. He eventually escaped to South Korea in 1950.

Figure 4.3 Kim Sung-Hi

In 1952, Kim Sung-Hi was invited to establish the Department of Psychiatry in Chonnam National University Medical School and Hospital in Gwangju. Unusually, declining university housing designated for professors, he lived in a room of the seventh ward of the university hospital. The seventh ward was the psychiatric ward that was an open ward. Kim Sung-Hi was the first psychiatrist who ran the psychiatric hospital as an open ward in Korea. During those days, Korean society had a strong prejudice against the mentally ill, and people criticised him for not locking them up and accused of himself being mad. His straightforward personality and critical stance towards inhumane prejudice against the mentally ill provoked further hostility of some colleagues against him. As a result, he was excluded from rehiring in 1976. Back in Seoul, he led a poor and solitary life until 1998 when a 'Kim Sung-Hi supporters' association' was formed by his former students who brought him back to Gwangju. After his return to Gwangju, for six years until his death, Kim Sung-Hi taught medical students, laid in bed, blind in one eye and only able to move his right hand. However, his students remembered him as having had an overwhelming and authoritative voice. He passed away on 31 December 2003.

Rhee Dong-Shick 이동식

Rhee Dong-Shick (1920–2014), a founder member of the Korean Neuropsychiatric Association, studied at the Daegu Medical School (1938–1941) and began studying psychiatry in 1942 at the Medical College of Kyungseong Imperial University. Pursuing the study of Kraepelinian psychiatry of the time, he also extensively read British, American and French psychiatry, as well as traditional Korean thoughts.

Figure 4.4 Rhee Dong-Shick

In 1954, he went to New York on the recommendation and encouragement of an American military psychiatrist to undertake a residency at the New York University Bellevue Medical Centre. While there he studied psychoanalysis at the William Alanson White Institute and engaged in twice-weekly psychoanalytic psychotherapy sessions. While studying psychoanalysis, Rhee Dong-Shick was also introduced to European philosophy, particularly phenomenology and existentialism. It was during this time that he discovered what he later called 'nuclear feeling'. He realised how Eastern ideas were valuable and significant within psychoanalysis and most importantly how Western psychoanalysis approaches the *Tao* of Eastern philosophy.

After four years of study in the United States, Rhee Dong-Shick visited Europe and attended international congresses, including the World Philosophers' Congress. Upon his return to Korea at the end of 1958, he introduced dynamic psychiatry, psychotherapy, interview techniques, as well as existential psychiatry to Korea. In the mid-1960s, he devoted his best efforts to studying the *Tao* including works of Buddhism, Confucianism, and the philosophers Lao-tzu and Chuang-tzu with prominent Korean monks and scholars. From then on, he maintained a serious, devoted practice of the *Tao* 도 (道; the Way). Later, he came to formulate a 'Taopsychotherapy' integrating the practices of *Tao* and psychotherapy.

Yu Seok-Jin 유석진

Yu Seok-Jin (1920–2008) graduated from the Medical College of Kyungseong Imperial University in 1944 and until 1985 he worked at this University which

Figure 4.5 Yu Seok-Jin

became the Seoul National University. Yu Seok-Jin, who operated a psychiatric clinic in the Seoul Juvenile Court in 1946, was always actively involved in developing programmes for child and juvenile mental health care. He was also the chief technical member operating the National Orphanage for Mental Defectives in 1949. In 1955, he opened 'St Peter Neuropsychiatric Clinic 베드루 신경정신과 의원' where he held his practice for 46 years. This is recorded as the first private clinic solely reserved for psychiatric treatment. In 1958, he participated in the inauguration of the Seoul Child Guidance Clinic. In 1960–1961, he took the lead in re-establishing the Korean Neuropsychiatric Association that had become little more than a name after the Korean War, by restoring its status and reinforcing its activities.

Yu Seok-Jin, in his earlier years, was devoted to reading psychoanalytic literature and teaching psychoanalysis, appealing to many Korean psychiatrists. With junior psychiatrists, he had translated some of Freud's works into Korean, but they disappeared during the Korean War. In his practice, Yu Seok-Jin was a pioneer in that he was the first to use so-called 'social scene therapy' by taking patients to outside markets, restaurants or theatres. Above all, his considerable contribution was to have introduced psychodrama, music, arts and dance into clinical practice. Already by the 1950s, he reported the efficacy of combining music with the traditional psychiatric treatment presenting in some of his cases. He who once owned a theatre that he willingly handed over to actors to use, was also a loyal advocate for talented, fragile poor artists including Lee Jung-Seob. As a pioneer of Korean psychiatry after the Liberation, he extensively expanded his work to incorporate dynamic psychiatry, psychoanalysis, military and pedopsychiatry, psychophysiology, psychodrama, music and art therapy.

Figure 4.6 Lee Jung-Seob 이중섭 (1916–1956) 'Ox 소': he is one of the most favourite and highly esteemed Korean artists, who suffered from a type of schizophrenia and was confined in several mental institutions around 1955 and died of hepatitis in 1956. Yu Seok-Jin was his doctor but also friend

Notes

1 At the time of opening, it was named 'Gwanghye-won 광혜원 (廣惠院, House of Extended Grace)' as a royal hospital. Within one month, it was renamed Jejung-won to reflect that it was also open for the general public.

2 The Severance hospital and medical school took the new name the Severance Union Medical College in 1913. It evolved to become the current Severance Hospital and Yonsei University College of Medicine in Seoul.

3 In 1938, there was an incident involving cheating on the college entrance exam. Prof. Choi Myung-Hak, a colleague of Lee Jung-Chul, revealed it to the faculty council and resigned. Lee Jung-Chul also submitted his resignation in sympathy with his colleague.

4 Rhi, B. Y. (2003). The roots of Korean psychiatry and its development. In T. Hamanaka & G. E. Berrios (Ed.), *Two Millennia of Psychiatry in West and East*. (pp. 95–106). Nagoya: Gakuju Shoin Publishers.

5 May 16 Coup: A military coup d'état in 1961, organised and carried out by General Park Jung-Hi and a group of soldiers under his command. Overthrowing the 2nd Republic, it installed the Military Revolutionary Committee. Park Jung-Hi led the autocratic government until he was assassinated in 1979.

6 There was also the belief originated by ancient Chinese philosophers that the liver was turned upside down in mental disease, and certain kinds of medication were used in the treatment to return the liver to its proper position. These medications were usually a plant poison which would cause the patient to have an attack of severe vomiting and diarrhoea. The medicine seemed to act upon the disease by changing the metabolism of the patient or by giving him or her chemical shock similar to the use of insulin or metrazol: extracted

from Yu, S. J. (1962). Mental disorders in the Korean rural communities. *Journal of the Korean Neuropsychiatric Association*, 1 (1), 9–27 (survey between 1956 and1960).

Bibliography

Lee, H.Y. (2004). Past, Present and Future of Korean Psychiatry. *Psychiatry Investigation Journal*, 1 (1), 9–13.

Lee, S. K., Lee, M. S., & Chung K. H. (Eds). (2004). *Life and Works of Professor Kim Sung-Hi Volume 2.* Seoul: Yiyu Publisher. [Korean]

Min, S. K. (2006). The past, present and future of psychopharmacology in Korea. *Clinical Psycho-pharmacology and Neuroscience*, 4, 11–23. [Korean]

Rhee, D. S. (1993). The Tao and Empathy: East Asian Interpretation. *Psychotherapy*,7 (1), 75–87.

Rhi, B. Y. (2003). The roots of Korean psychiatry and its development. In T. Hamanaka & G. E. Berrios (Ed.), *Two Millennia of Psychiatry in West and East.* (pp. 95–106). Nagoya: Gakuju Shoin Publishers.

Salman, A. (Ed.). (2006). *Freud and the Far East: Psychoanalytic perspectives on the people and culture of China, Japan, and Korea.* Lanham, MD: Jason Aronson.

Yeo, I. S. (2008). The establishment of SUMC (Severance Union Medical College) psychiatry department & the formation of humanistic tradition. *Korean Journal of Medical History*, 17 (1), 57–74. [Korean]

Yeo, I. S. (2009). Basic Medical Science in Jejungwon and the SUMC 1885–1945. *Yonsei Journal of Medical History*, 12 (1), 43–58. [Korean]

Yu, S. J. (1962). Mental Disorders in the Korean Rural Communities. *Journal of the Korean Neuropsychiatric Association*,1 (1), 9–27.

5 Influence from clinical psychology

Introduction of psychology: 1910s–1945

Western psychology as a modern science was introduced through American missionaries as a branch of biology in the latter part of the Joseon era around 1907. It was taught at private institutions of the Christian system such as Ewha Haktang (est. 1886, the first woman's modern education institution, later Ewha Woman's University 이화여자대학); Yonhui College (est. 1915, originally as Joseon Christian College, developed into Yonsei University 연세대학); and Chung-Ang Child Education (est. 1928, later Chung-Ang University 중앙대학).

According to an entry in the *Hwangsung* newspaper 황성신문 dated 7 September 1908, which published the list of classes taught at the Ewha Haktang 이화학당, psychology was established as a regular curriculum at the institution as early as 1908. During the colonial period (1910–1945), the Ewha Haktang continued to offer classes on psychology which was the functional psychology

Figure 5.1 Lower grade girls, Ewha Haktang, 1908/1922 © 2014 University of Southern California

favoured by Christian systems. At the Yonhui College 연희전문학교, Lee Gwan-Yong 이관용 (1894–1933), the first Korean to receive a doctorate in philosophy at Zürich University in 1923 (thesis title: 'Will as basic fact of Consciousness'), taught psychology using a textbook in Japanese during the 1920s. Around the same period, at the Chung-Ang Child Education 중앙유아사범과, Hong Byung-Seon 홍병선 (1888–1967), a Methodist minister and YMCA activist, taught child psychology using a textbook *Early Childhood Psychology* that he published in 1922 with the support of American missionaries.

In 1924, the Kyungseong Imperial University (KIU) offered psychology in the Department of Philosophy as a major study programme for training psychologists. Until the Liberation (1945), it was the only regular training programme of psychology. Most professors of the KIU were Japanese psychologists who studied at Wundt's Laboratory at the University of Leipzig or in the Department of Philosophy at the Berlin University, and inherited the German academic tradition. Consequently, psychology in Korea during this period was dominated by German experimental psychology. Mental illness was more or less treated as physical illness and clinical aspects of psychology barely existed.

Six Koreans majored in psychology at the KIU under the colonial government: Im Seok-Jae, Youn Tae-Rim, Lee Jin-Sook, Lee Eui-Chul, Lee Bon-Nyung and Seo Myung-Won. Four Korean psychologists were trained abroad before the Liberation: Lee Jae-Wan, Sung Baek-Seon, Go Soon-Deok and Bang Hyun-Mo. Among them, Lee Bon-Nyung 이본녕 who established the Department of Psychology at the Chung-Ang University and introduced Social Psychology, and Lee Jae-Wan 이재완 who was formerly a professor at the College of Education of the SNU and studied at the University of California and went to North Korea during the war. Lee Bon-Nyung and Lee Jae-Wan were working at the SNU when the war broke out and the North Korean armies arrived in Seoul. Lee Bon-Nyung who helped them went to North Korea, whereas Lee Jae-Wan was kidnapped in 1952. Whether his abduction was directly connected with Lee Bon-Nyung is unknown. Go Soon-Deok 고순덕 (1917–1990) found permanent residency in America after obtaining a doctorate in psychology at Harvard University in 1954. On the other hand, Im Seok-Jae 임석재 (1903–1998) who was the first Korean whose major was psychology (1924–1930) and taught educational psychology at the SNU became more known as an eminent folklorist, while Seo Myung-Won 서명원 (1919–2006) dedicated more to the development of pedagogy, after receiving a doctorate in education at the George Peabody College of Education in America. Therefore, the number of Korean psychologists who were active in Korea by the time of the Liberation was five.

Among the group of KIU graduates, Lee Jin-Sook 이진숙 (1908–1962) was the only person who obtained the position of research assistant in the psychology section around 1933. Until he passed away from a chronic illness in 1962, he dedicated himself to the training of young psychologists, contributing to starting clinical psychology at the SNU. Youn Tae-Rim 윤태림 (1908–1991) contributed to the establishment of the 'Korean Counsellors' Association (est. 1963)' and the development of clinical and counselling psychology. He was the first domestic doctorate of psychology at the SNU with the thesis titled 'The Personality of Koreans' in 1965. Youn Tae-Rim published 14 books including *Introduction to Psychology* (1958) and *Youth Psychology* (1959). Lee Eui-Chul 이의철 (?–1997) helped to create the division of clinical psychology under the Korean Psychological Association (est. 1946) in 1964. Sung Baek-Seon 성백선 (1914–1977), who studied at the Waseda University between 1937 and 1940, established the Department of Psychology at the Sung-Kyun-Kwan University 성균관대학 in 1953 and at the Korea University 고려대학 in 1955. Having a keen interest in industrial psychology, he collected thousands of test data to standardise 'The Uchida-Kraepelin (U-K) Test'. Bang Hyun-Mo 방현모 (1919–1990), who obtained a doctorate at the Tohoku University Japan in 1941, taught at the Chung-Ang and then the Sung-Kyun-Kwan University. These people played the principle roles in the renaissance of Korean psychology after the Liberation. In these early days, the focus was mostly on education and research related to basic psychology.

Amongst those who did not major in psychology but taught psychology during this period, there was notably Han Chi-Jin 한치진 (1910–?), a philosopher and sociologist who received a doctorate in Philosophy at the University of Southern California in 1928. He joined the Ewha Haktang in 1933 and offered psychology lectures until 1936. He produced more than 33 books including *Introduction to New Psychology* 신심리학개론 (1930) and *Theory of Personality Psychology* 인격심리학원론 (1939) and hundreds of articles covering philosophy, religion, political science, sociology and psychology until his kidnapping[1] to North Korea in 1950 during the Korean War.

Early development of clinical psychology: 1946–1970s

In February 1946, on the Lunar New Year's Day, the Korean psychologists who had trained during the colonial period assembled (with the exception of Youn

Figure 5.2 Im Seok-Jae, Han Chi-Jin, Lee Jin-Sook

Tae-Rim who had switched careers to become a judge after studying law, and Lee Eui-Chul who was unreachable), and they founded the 'Joseon Psychological Association 조선심리학회'. It was renamed the 'Daehan Psychological Association 대한심리학회' in 1949 and then the 'Korean Psychological Association 한국심리학회' in 1953. In September 1946, the Department of Psychology within the College of Arts and Sciences was inaugurated at Seoul National University. The original faculty consisted of Lee Bon-Nyung, Go Soon-Deok and Lee Jin-Sook who played the most crucial role in the development of psychology at the SNU. Each taught respectively: Pavlov's 'Conditioned Reflex', Kimball's 'Social Psychology' and Koehler's 'Gestalt Psychology'; Woodwords's 'Experimental Psychology', Child Psychology and Guildford's 'Psychological Measurement and Statistics'; Hilgard's 'Introduction to Psychology' while focusing on sensory experiments. A year later in 1947, the Department of Psychology was established at the Chung-Ang University. These two departments and the Joseon Psychological Association made significant contributions to the early development of psychology.

After the Liberation, American military psychologists attached to the US Military Government administration introduced Korean psychologists to intelligence tests and new fields of educational, industrial and clinical psychology. At that time, most Korean psychologists were still very much under the influence of the German psychology of Wundt, Koffka and Kohler, and ideologically unsympathetic towards American approaches to psychology. They ignored such applied fields by academic preference. An exception was Sung Baek-Seon who already in 1946, had been operating 'Consultation Services for Problem Children 문제아동자문기관' supported by a social welfare agency.

During this period, an American citizen and doctorate in psychology (1931) from the University of Chicago, Yeom Gwang-Seob 염광섭 served as Educational Adviser in the US Military Government between 1946 and 1948. During this brief period, he also gave lectures on Psychological tests and Statistics at the SNU. Most Korean psychologists considered that the knowledge obtained by statistical methods was merely of a probabilistic assessment and hardly legitimate, and thus invaluable. On the other hand, Lee Jin-Sook and Go Soon-Deok were inspired by his lectures and took the opportunity to gain new understanding about the functionalism of American psychology. They pursued research accepting its tenets after the war. By introducing American psychology, which had previously only been understood conceptually by Korean psychologists, Yeom Gwang-Seob played an active part during the formative period of psychology and made a significant contribution to the early development of Korean clinical psychology.

Beginning of clinical psychology: 1950s

Psychology in Korea before the Liberation had few ties with American functional psychology but took a new turn during the war. During the Korean War, American and Korean psychologists fighting as psychological warfare agents, produced psychological evaluations and researches for the military, in which psychological assessment tools such as Wechsler-Bellevue Intelligence Scale, MMPI and Rorschach test were used to examine the intellectual and psychological stability of conscripted soldiers. Consequently, the Korean War became the catalyst for the dawn of clinical psychology in Korea and promoted, together with the social need for applied psychology, clinical psychology research and activities after the war.

Around this time, two new psychology departments were created at the Ewha Woman's University in 1951 and the Sung-Kyun-Kwan University in 1954. After the war, interest in clinical psychology gradually increased among psychologists, and clinical psychology began being taught at these psychology departments. At the SNU, Lee Jin-Sook, who had initially led the academic traditions of experimental psychology under the influence of German psychology at the KIU, after participating in psychological evaluations and researches during the war, from 1954 began offering classes such as 'Personality Psychology' which was closely related to clinical psychology. He released various writings including 'Introduction of Psychology (1949)'; 'Wechsler-Bellevue Intelligence Scale (1953, co-authored with Go Soon-Deok); 'Personality Test (1959)', 'Introduction of Early Childhood Psychology (1956)'; 'Freud (1961)'; and 'Modern Psychology (1962, translation of 'Contemporary Schools of Psychology' of Woodworth).

Furthermore, Lee Jin-Sook made a significant change around 1960 by opening an applied psychology course named 'Team-work'. Emphasising collaboration with neighbouring fields, this 'Team-work' course consisted of the ensemble of lectures on clinical psychology, abnormal psychology, psychopathology, case work and group work. Some of the SNU graduates who followed his courses at this time later took leading roles in the development of clinical psychology in Korea. It was a great loss for his students, as well as for the development of clinical psychology, when Lee Jin-Sook passed away in 1962 amid the wave of enthusiasm of innovation. On the other hand, towards the late 1950s, Youn Tae-Rim, who had taken a law degree after having studied psychology and had been working as a judge for a while, returned to the field of psychology and started giving lectures on clinical psychology. Further, the Department of Psychology at the Korea University was inaugurated in 1959 under the direction of Sung Baek-Seon. This department has been the repository of Korean clinical psychology.

Children's Advisory Board 1958

The outstanding achievement of the 1950s was the establishment of the 'Children's Advisory Board' in 1958, the predecessor of the 'Seoul Child Counselling Centre 서울아동상담소'. For the first time, a group of experts from different fields gathered and ran a clinic for consultation. It consisted of a lawyer Gwon Soun-Young, a psychologist Sung Baek-Seon, a psychiatrist Yu Seok-Jin and a social worker Ha Sang-Rak. The team met for a weekly conference at which intake cases were presented for diagnosis and treatment planning, and education for the general public was also discussed. During the first 18 months, it had about 228 cases, demonstrating a growing acceptance of psychiatric services by the public. There was financial support from some willing citizens. Newspaper publishers also assisted by providing space for articles on case studies and other relevant information about the clinic or mental hygiene, in general. Its success stimulated the Ministry of Education to adopt the establishment of school guidance counselling services for every school and the Ministry of Justice to run a juvenile delinquency programme. The Children's Advisory Board was the first collaboration of mental health teams raising awareness of mental health from the late 1950s on.

Growth of clinical psychology: 1960s–1970s

In 1958–1959, Lee Ji-Young who had graduated from the Ewha Woman's University majoring in educational psychology carried out Rorschach tests in domestic relation courts. In 1959, she gave the Rorschach test to patients at the Seoul National University Medical School and became the first psychologist to practise in a psychiatric department. Between 1961 and 1967, each year the Defence Ministry selected an army officer with a psychology or education major and sent them to the Walter-Reed American Army Hospital for an internship of six months. On their return, they served in the Korean Army Hospitals as clinical psychology army officers. Among them were Han Myung-Taek, Won Ho-Taek, Won Ho-Shick and Kim Chul-Soo. Won Ho-Taek on his return from the internship in 1963 brought with him the original Wechsler, MMPI, Rorschach, Thematic Apperception Test, Bender-Gestalt and Sentence Completion Test. Now retired from the Army, these first 'state-authorised' clinical psychologists were appointed at psychiatric hospitals and medical schools.

In addition, a number of psychiatrists, mostly influenced by American dynamic psychiatry, started to work together with clinical psychologists in clinical settings. Subsequently, more clinical psychologists began working in psychiatric hospitals as mental health experts in the 1960s. In 1962, Ahn Ga-Hee who had graduated from the Ewha Woman's University began working full-time as a clinical psychologist at the Seoul National (Mental) Hospital 국립정신병원 which inaugurated the independent department of clinical psychology. In 1963, a SNU graduate, Lee Hyun-Soo was appointed as the head of this department. This was significant in a sense that clinical psychologists were officially recognised as independent professionals by the Ministry of Health and Social Affairs. In 1963, Kim Jung-Soul started working as a clinical psychologist at Myungdong St Mary's Hospital 명동성모병원 of the Catholic University Medical School 가톨릭의대. In the same year, Sudo Medical School (predecessor of Korea University Medical School) opened the 'Neurosis Counselling Centre' and Shin Dong-Kyun, who had graduated from the SNU, was appointed as its clinical psychologist. Won Ho-Taek in 1965 and Won Ho-Shick in 1966 started working full-time as clinical psychologists at Daegu Neuropsychiatric Clinic and Chungtangri-Nowoe

Figure 5.3 Seoul National Mental Hospital (est. 1962) © 2008 Voice of People

Hospital respectively. Gradually clinical psychologists consolidated their position in the field. These clinical psychologists were wholly in charge of psychological diagnoses using psychological tests. Projective tests of Draw-A-Person Test, Rorschach and Thematic Apperception Test were mostly used until the Korean versions of Wechsler for adults and MMPI were published in 1963. Some also used the translated Sentence Completion Test. In the 1970s clinical psychologists gradually had opportunities to learn and practise psychotherapy.

Society of clinical psychology 1964

As more psychologists began to work in psychiatric clinical fields, the need for education and training to improve the qualifications of clinical psychologists became critical. To meet these practical demands, the Korean Psychological Association (KPA est. 1946) organised a separate division, the 'Society of Clinical Psychology' in 1964 (later in 1987 this developed into the 'Korean Clinical Psychology Association'). Since 1967, the Society of Clinical Psychology has published the *Korean Journal of Clinical Psychology* in which various case studies and theories are shared and discussed. The KPA made further efforts to stipulate the eligibility regulation and licence for clinical psychologists in order to produce clinical psychology experts. Subsequently, the KPA enacted the regulations for qualification as a professional clinical psychologist in 1971. The first certification exam was conducted in February 1973 and seven persons got through the exam. In October of the same year, these seven clinical psychologists were awarded the KPA Certificate for Clinical Psychology Professional, opening the first generation of veritable Korean psychologists. They were Kim Seong-Tae, Lee Hyun-Soo, Kim Jung-Soul, Shin Dong-Kyun, Han Myung-Taek, Yeom Tae-Ho and Won Ho-Taek. Since then, the KPA holds an annual certifying examination thereby helping majors in psychology to advance into society.

As academic bases for the professionalisation of clinical psychology steadily formed, graduate courses for master's degrees in clinical psychology appeared starting with the Korea University in the mid-1960s. Since 1973, clinical psychologists with masters have come forth in great numbers. In the 1970s, a doctoral programme in clinical psychology was offered at the Korea University and the Seoul National University. A number of psychologists with doctoral degrees obtained mostly in the United States also started to appear on the scene in the 1970s. They worked together with home-trained psychologists to reshape psychology in Korea making it more professionally oriented and viable. During this period, an internship programme, albeit very limited, began for graduate students. Since that time, clinical psychology has become firmly established as an applied field within psychology that integrates scientific methods and professional service.

First psychotherapy by clinical psychologist 1966

In 1965, Won Ho-Taek 원호택 (1935–) started teaching psychological assessments at the Kyungbuk University Medical School, while still working at the Army Hospital. The same year, he retired from the Army as a clinical psychology army officer and started working at the Daegu Neuropsychiatric Clinic held by a psychiatrist, Jung Chang-Young, while continuing teaching at the Kyungbuk University Medical School. Around this period, together with psychiatric residents from the Kyungbuk University, he took part in the dynamic group therapy facilitated by Jung Chang-Young for six months. Subsequently, through the solicitude of Jung Chang-Young, Won Ho-Taek began offering group therapy for inpatients, mostly the schizophrenics, and individual therapy for outpatients at the Daegu Neuropsychiatric Clinic, while his main duty at the clinic remained giving psychological diagnosis and evaluation. This was significant as it was the first time that a non-psychiatric doctor had provided both group and individual psychotherapy. This experience became a pillar for his further career as a clinical psychologist, researcher and psychotherapist.

In 1971, Won Ho-Taek moved to the Kyunghee University Medical School 경희의대. Under the auspices of psychiatrist Kim Gwang-Il 김광일 who was in charge of the psychiatric department, he provided group and individual psychotherapy, while working as an assistant professor of clinical psychology. This was unconventional at that time when psychotherapy was exclusive to psychiatrists especially within the context of medical school. In 1975, they both moved to the Hanyang University Medical School 한양의대 where Won Ho-Taek installed the mental health research centre and the internship programme of three-year training for clinical psychology professionals in 1976. Around this time, adopting methods of reality therapy, behavioural therapy and person-centred therapy, he pursued an eclectic approach to psychotherapy, gradually focusing more on a cognitive behavioural approach.

Expansion of clinical psychology: 1980s–

Professional independence: 1980s–1990s

At the turn of 1980s, psychodynamic psychiatry declined and the focus began to rapidly turn towards biological psychiatry. Researches in neuroscience and psychopharmacology became particularly active and more psychiatrists adopted the view of psychopathology in the prospect of brain nerve system disease. Moreover, Korean psychiatrists became wary and took a negative position on psychotherapy by psychologists after they witnessed the speedy growth of clinical psychologists in the United States. They put up their guard against them so as not to lose their privilege as the sole professional conducting psychotherapy. As a result, fewer psychologists had their positions at the hospitals renewed and those that remained had their functions reduced to mostly psychological assessment. The preference for psychotherapy in psychiatric hospitals was disappearing and lots of hospitals no longer allowed psychologists to practise psychotherapy. In this regard, the 1980s was the era of identity crisis for Korean psychologists. Within these conditions, clinical psychologists took measures to strike out on a path of their own expertise. They started to open private psychotherapy centres offering mostly cognitive behavioural therapy which became the preferred method amongst clinical psychologists in the 1980s. Continued expansion was seen during the 1980s along with the influx of psychological research. At the beginning of the 1990s, private practice activities and areas of their expertise noticeably increased. This was further accelerated by the promulgation of legislation on mental health in the late 1990s.

Mental Health Act 1997

The Mental Health Act 정신보건법 that was passed by Parliament in December 1995 became effective in 1997. The basic principle of the act was assuring dignity and value as a human being, fair treatment and prohibition of unjust discrimination for everyone with mental illness. It essentially promoted prevention, treatments and rehabilitation of mental illness through increasing mental health facilities, awareness and professionalism. Since the enactment, the Ministry of Health and Social Affairs (MHSA) 보건복지부 has provided the national licence to clinical psychologists, 'Mental Health Clinical Psychologist 정신보건임상심리사' to accommodate these needs. Nevertheless, albeit this enforcement, there has been no significant change in reality for the status of psychologists in the field. The Korean Clinical Psychology Association (KCPA) has continued to autonomously issue the state-recognised certificate for 'Clinical Psychology Professional 임상심리전문가' trying to maintain their professional standards and fight for equal treatment with doctors. In 2002, the Human Resources Development Service of Korea started up the 'National Technical Qualification of Clinical Psychologists'. It aimed to train professional officers for counselling and rehabilitation to meet the needs of the national policy to prevent a variety of social problems, to protect and promote public health and to improve the quality of life of individuals. Currently, these three state-certificated qualifications for clinical psychologists are issued by the three different organisations. Recently, the qualification issued by the Human Resources Development Service lost effect and most young clinical psychologists now obtain a Mental Health Clinical Psychologist's certificate of MHSA after an internship and exam. More experienced clinical psychologists become certified in the Clinical Psychology Professional of KCPA.

Development of expertise: 2000s

In the past, clinical psychologists primarily worked at universities as professors, counsellors for students or consultants and at hospitals offering psychological diagnosis and evaluation in the psychiatric department. Since the late 1990s, an increasing number of clinical psychologists have been working as professionals in private mental health centres or in government organisations, for example, the National Human Rights Commission of Korea, the National Youth Commission, the Fact-finding Committee for Mysterious Deaths in the Military, the Family Court, the National Police Agency, probation offices, prisons and public schools. Particularly in recent years, clinical psychologists are largely acknowledged for their performance in rehabilitation programmes for chronic mental disabilities by effectively applying cognitive behavioural group therapy with them. Increasingly, clinical psychologists are also involved in implanting structured programmes targeted at the specific patient groups of social phobia, panic disorder or obsessive compulsive disorders in which cognitive behavioural therapy is extensively used. They are equally active in family or public education, raising awareness and consciousness on mental health issues.

By 2012, 800 members of the Korean Clinical Psychology Association had obtained the certificate for Clinical Psychology Professional after completing their internships. In addition, the number of persons who had acquired the licence for Mental Health Clinical Psychologist offered by the Ministry of Health and Social Affairs had reached around 2,000. These clinical psychologists have constantly expanded the sphere of their activities. For the last decade in particular, they have taken a profound interest in developing new fields for their expertise, and behavioural medicine, paediatric psychology and forensic psychology have emerged as prospective areas. At the present time, clinical psychologists and mental health social workers are the only two mental health professionals, except for psychiatric doctors and nurses, who are certified by the Korean government legislation, and clinical psychologist is the only non-medical mental health professional who can obtain a national certificate to deliver psychotherapeutic treatment to mentally ill people in Korea.

Note

1 After the Liberation, Han Chi-Jin was an active porte-parole for the democracy. His family and colleagues believe this was a major reason for his abduction by the Communists. The family has not heard from him since the abduction. During the Korean War, about 95,000 Koreans were abducted to North Korea. They include leaders in all sectors of the society, intellectuals, engineers and young people.

Bibliography

Cha, J. H. (1978). Korean Psychology: A Survey of a science and profession. *Journal of Korean Social Science*, 5 (1), 142–184. [Korean]

Cha, J. H. (2005). The Development and present of psychology in Korea. *Journal of Korean Social Science*, 27(1, 2), 167–184. [Korean]

Won, H. T. (2000). Four decades of clinical psychology in Korea. *Psychological Science*, 9(1), 1–13. [Korean]

Won, H. T., & Yeom, T. H. (1986). A brief history of clinical psychology in Korea. *Journal of Behavioural Sciences*, 8 (1), 109–117.

Yu, S. J. (1962). Progress in care & treatment of mental illness in Korea. *Journal of Korean Neuropsychiatric Association*,1 (1), 55–62.

6 Counselling development

The Korean society of the post-1950s marked an era of profound social structural development. Koreans were desperate to overcome poverty and oppression. Their exceptional eagerness for success, and education in particular promoting openness to Western influences, led Korea to rapid industrialisation and modernisation. It accelerated the transition from a traditional to the modern society of Korea. However, Korea was lacking a solid foundation to effect its smooth transition from traditional to modern society. Consequently, this produced confusion, uncertainty and tension within Korean society provoking cross-societal and mental disequilibrium. Under the circumstances, many suffered in one form or another without much intervention from the government or mental health community. A major impetus for intervention came forth, instead, from both schools and churches which recognised the necessity to provide counselling and training of counsellors. Therefore, Korea's counselling history is closely related to its educational history on the one hand, and to Christianity on the other hand.

In addition to school and pastoral counselling, most distinctively rehabilitation counselling, which has a relatively brief history in Korea, has grown rapidly since its inception in the early 1990s, and has continued to prosper in recent years. Career counselling has also widely expanded in Korea. The growing flexibility of career changes since the late 1990s has served as the impetus for the increased attention towards persons with career-related issues. Counselling for domestic affairs such as divorce, domestic violence and child abuse has equally increased. The Anti-domestic Violence Counselling Programme provided by the 'Korea Legal Aid Centre for Family Relations 한국 가정법률 상담소' is one of the leading services in this area, and it has now more than 32 branches in the country. They offer programmes comprised of individual, couple and group counselling, as well as educational lectures and camps for married couples. More facilities such as 'Women Crisis Centres 여성 위기상담소' and 'Women's Shelters' for battered women and their children have emerged. The growing number of such centres reflects the seriousness of domestic violence and abuse in contemporary Korean society. Recently, computer-mediated communication has offered another mode of counselling, and there are numerous websites which offer virtual counselling and computerised assessment. Computer-based counselling has created a new pool of patients who have not in the past sought person-to-person counselling services.

Early counselling psychology: 1950s–1970s

The Western model of counselling was introduced into Korea during the postwar period by American delegates of education in the process of initiating the new education movement. They taught Korean educators counselling methods along with American education ideas and practices, John Dewey's child-centred education and pragmatism in particular. Typically, the counselling during this period was characterised by an emphasis on child welfare and the emotional, social adjustment and development of adolescents. The 'Children's Advisory Board' inaugurated in 1958, heralding the first set of counselling activities in Korea, stimulated the Ministry of Education to adopt the establishment of school guidance counselling services for every school. As a result, between 1958 and 1961, about 170 secondary teachers were trained as part-time counsellors, then called 'disciplinary guidance teachers'. The missionaries from the United States who got involved early in education then set about the establishment of schools, equally reinforcing their educational and evangelical work, expanding the churches and their involvement in Korean society during the 1950s. In the 1960s, the number of Christians dramatically grew and church organisations became increasingly active in undertaking various social services, providing guidance and counselling, as well as material aids. Gradually, pastoral counselling emerged gaining recognition in Korea.

Entering the 1960s, college professors of psychology and education began to explore counselling concepts and set up counselling activities. The opening of the 'Student Guidance Centre' at the Seoul National University in 1962 was crucial in the development of counselling in Korea, serving as a primary nest for the founding of professional counselling. In 1963, the 'Korean Counsellors' Association (KCA) 한국 카운셀러 협회' was founded consisting of school counsellors and college professionals. Youn Tae-Rim who worked as a director of the Student Guidance Centre in the mid-1960s took the central role to establish the KCA which he headed until 1972. The inauguration of KCA was significant in that it was the first professional organisation for school counsellors and activated the counselling movement. Since its launch, the KCA has been the pivotal point in developing and sustaining the professionalism of counsellors, through providing forums for discussion of new researches in counselling theories and case studies. Nonetheless, in the 1960s, theories and practices of counselling were not well established and most counsellors commonly faced role confusion of not knowing precisely what to do.

In the 1970s, counselling theories and resources were more systematically organised, and counselling began to emerge as a profession. There were increasing efforts to secure the expertise of counselling. In 1972, the first major master's course in counselling was opened at the Ewha Woman's University. In 1973, the 'Korean Psychological Association (KPA)' conducted its first certification exam and six counselling psychologists were awarded with the certificate: Kim Ki-Seok,

Lee Sang-Ro, Choi Jung-Hoon, Jin Wi-Gyo, Hong Seong-Hwa and Han Deok-Ung. In 1976, the Korean College Counselling Academy opened providing a wide range of workshops, seminars and training programmes, and introduced various therapeutic theories. Group counselling programmes such as sensitivity training and T-group were used in practice. Around this period, many Korean scholars also went abroad for further education. Upon their return from their foreign training, they brought with them Western approaches to counselling. Theories of psychoanalytical, behavioural and humanistic counselling were introduced and various workshops and seminars were held throughout the country. The field of counselling rapidly expanded and many people have been actively involved and trained. Gradually, counselling began to be perceived as a viable approach to helping individuals cope with various psychological problems.

SNU Student Guidance Centre 1962 학생지도연구소

The SNU Student Guidance Centre opened in 1962 led by professors of education. With the opening of Student Guidance Centre, professors of education and psychology departments started offering training programmes and internship, as well as counselling services, to university students. For the first time they introduced 'counselling psychology' into Korea. Many psychology and education graduates, who took part in the internship programmes, played a leading role in the development of counselling psychology. During this time, the theory of Carl Rogers was taught and researched. When his book *Counselling and Psychotherapy* (1942) was translated into Korean in 1963, his non-directive counselling methodology almost immediately became the dominant counselling methodology. Counselling psychology was taught as a separate division of study and counselling psychologists or counsellors[1] independently conducted psychotherapy. In 1968, Lee Chang-Ho, one of pioneers of counselling psychology in Korea, took full charge of the Centre and the counselling services became much more structured. Kim Ki-Seok who was the first counselling psychologist certified by the Korean Psychological Association in 1973, took the lead in developing the Centre as the matrix of student guidance and counselling in the universities in Korea which sprang up thereafter. Another person who made a great contribution was Rhee Dong-Shick. He was the only psychiatrist during this period who exceptionally and willingly offered training and supervision to many leading psychologists with a psychotherapeutic orientation, strengthening ties between psychologists and psychiatrists.

Counselling development: 1980s–

A number of textbooks related to counselling emerged from the 1980s. Various counselling theories and ideologies introduced in the 1970s by the foreign-trained Korean educators and psychologists were extensively taught across Korea during this period. The 'Korea Counselling Centre 한국 심리상담 연구소'

Figure 6.1 SNU Student Guidance Centre © 1962 SNU

(est. 1986, by Kim In-Za) and many other academic associations and professional organisations were also established. They designed and implemented new counselling programmes – personal growth groups, human relations training, assertiveness training or family enrichment programmes in various settings. The LoveAid Helpline Centre opened in 1981 offering the first 24-hour counselling service. Juvenile delinquency was on the rise around this period. The liberalisation of the hair and dress code of middle and high school students in 1982 was definitely a contributing factor. It led to an increased need for youth counselling, and governmental institutions and social organisations started opening counselling centres.

In 1987, counselling psychology, initially housed in the division of clinical psychology, achieved its independence and created a separate division within the Korean Psychological Association, 'Counselling Psychology and Psychotherapy Association'. This was renamed the 'Korean Counselling Psychological Association (KCPA) 한국 상담심리 학회' in 2003. Since the creation of the division, the field of counselling psychology has witnessed tremendous growth. In 1989, the KCPA launched its first volume of a major new empirical journal, the *Korean Journal of Counselling and Psychotherapy*. It has been also providing qualifications for the 'Counselling Psychologist Certificates' to foster competent counsellors and provide professional certificates to qualified counselling professionals since its first award in 1973.

In the 1990s and the 2000s, both academic manuscripts on counselling and professional associations significantly increased. Many regional and national conferences and workshops related to the practice of counselling took place throughout the country. As counselling was increasingly accepted by the government, a growing number of government-sponsored public counselling institutions were established. Privately funded counselling centres also sprang up everywhere.

The places where counsellors work became more varied. In 2002, a national qualification for youth counsellor was initiated stimulating active support on youth counselling at the national level. An increasing number of graduates are now finding positions at Youth counselling centres, as well as university counselling centres, communicates, social organisations, religious institutions, workplaces, the military or the court. With now over 60 years of history, the profession of counselling in Korea has been growing rapidly in recent years and the numbers of counsellors and their workplaces continue to grow. Currently, over 800 privately funded counselling centres exist in Korea and the number is mounting. The KPA which granted certificates to only six counsellors in 1973 when the certification system began has today more than 4,000 members attempting to become certified counsellors, and the number has been increasing each year. In March 2011, the number of people who obtained the 'Counselling Psychologist Certificate' swelled to over 2,900. The establishment of 'Korean Counselling Association (KCA) 한국상담학회' in 2000 accelerated the expansion of counselling further. Both certificates granted by the KCPA and the KCA are widely recognised as an official qualification and the certified counsellors obtain greater public recognition as professionals in the field.

Despite its outstanding growth, Korean counselling psychology, however, still struggles to define its own identity today. The members of KCPA have sought to make a strong move towards the creation of government licences. However, the Ministry of Health and Welfare which certifies clinical psychologists and social workers, still argues that although counsellors provide a variety of important services, their professional roles and boundaries are not well defined, and they do not yet qualify for legal licensing as a profession. Moreover, Korean counsellors struggle to retain a position in a highly competitive environment contending for limited places with professionals of other disciplines such as clinical psychologists and social workers, and more recently with social psychologists or developmental psychologists. In particular, many clinical psychologists who mostly secured positions in hospitals are now increasingly turning to private practices because of the overflow of clinical psychologists and the limited positions in hospital. They widely provide counselling services to the general populace. Social psychologists and developmental psychologists also claim their qualifications as practitioners, providing counselling to certain sectors of the population including infants and children, or criminals at correction centres.

Even though there are no government licences for counsellors in Korea yet, and despite the challenges inherent in aggressive and incessant competition for developing the profession, there is no doubt that Korean counsellors are currently playing multiple roles as significant helping professionals for mental health in contemporary Korean society. With a profound sense of duty to enhance their professional practices to provide a basis for the overall quality of life of Korean people, they continue to grow, solidifying their professionalism. Furthermore, many Koreans who are reluctant to consult psychiatrists or clinical psychologists in medical hospital settings, mostly because of the stigmatisation associated with mental disorders, being 'crazy', would instead seek help from counsellors in counselling centres which are actively beginning to accommodate this need. In particular, parents having their children consulted for their psychological or behavioural issues would prefer to seek non-medical counsellors or psychotherapists to avoid leaving behind any medical records of mental treatments in the medical history of their children. Hence, today, counsellors remain the most active but above all, the most accessible group among all mental health practitioners as practising in the most diverse range of clinical settings. Over the years, Korean counsellors have developed different ways to form a collaborative therapeutic alliance with patients. Since the 1990s, Korean professors and counsellors have also begun to explore counselling concepts and have striven to establish counselling activities more appropriate for Korean people. They have been attempting to integrate traditional psychotherapeutic techniques from Korean Shamanism, Buddhism and Taoism into the counselling process. Lee Chang-Ho played leading role in shaping this field.

Lee Chang-Ho 이장호

Lee Chang-Ho (1936–) studied at Seoul National University (SNU) and Texas University, and taught and worked at SNU and the SNU Student Guidance Centre. As the tenth counselling psychologist certified by the Korean Psychological Association, he has been the leading figure in the development of counselling psychology in Korea. He has published many articles, case studies and books including *The Introduction of Counselling Psychology*. Lee Chang-Ho developed a method of counselling in which he integrated the mode of meditation and yoga. He called his method 'Integral Counselling 통합상담' and defined it as an eclectic, synthetic, proactive approach. It uses Western counselling techniques of person-centred, gestalt or cognitive behavioural therapies, while its aim is placed on reaching the *Tao* by training both body and mind. In his integral counselling, most of all, it is important to notice the state of body and mind at here and now, and patients usually sit still for about 5–10 minutes both at the beginning and before the ending of each session. They are also given homework of keeping a journal of each session. In the same way, the integral counselling for groups is carried out usually beginning with yoga and meditation to enhance attention. Lee Chang-Ho, with his integral counselling, encouraged patients to make meditation a way of life, urging them to switch focus from a 'doing' to a 'being' of each moment to relieve psychological pains. In 2001, he took part in launching 'Hankyore Counselling Centre 한겨레 상담센터' as a branch agency of the Korean Counselling Psychology Association. In 2006, he opened the 'Integral Counselling Institute' and continues to diffuse the integral counselling by training and supervising young counsellors through case studies.

School counselling

School counselling in Korea was established in the process of liquidating the Japanese colonial education system after the Liberation, and in the pursuit of 'new education' as part of democratising the educational system in the 1950s. A specialised UN agency, UNESCO-UNKRA Educational Delegation initiated educational missions in Korea. During their three visits from 1952 to 1962, they taught Korean educators about new counselling and guidance theories and methods, diverting them from the disciplinarian approaches, such as corporal punishment, in use at that time. The Seoul City Education Committee took the initiative in 1958 to produce 47 school counsellors, called them 'disciplinary guidance teachers', who served to guide problematic students and improve educational methodologies in public and private schools. About 170 disciplinary guidance teachers produced during this period of inception of counselling between 1958 and 1961 played a pivotal role in the further development of counselling in Korea. Around this time, Rogers's non-directive counselling theory was introduced and effectively applied in youth counselling, also activating the establishment of student counselling centres at universities. This initiative of the Seoul City Education Committee promoted further movements that resulted in the 1963 Education Act from the Ministry of Education (now the Ministry of Education, Science and Technology). The 1963 Education Act stated that all middle and high schools should have disciplinary guidance teachers. In cooperation with the Central Education Research Institute, the Ministry of Education held seminars and training sessions on student guidance and counselling in the school system, and produced many disciplinary guidance teachers and counselling training programmes. The title of disciplinary guidance teacher was changed into 'career counselling teacher' in 1990, there being no major difference in terms of their roles.

In December 1963, the Korean Counsellors' Association (KCA) was set up by school counsellors and college professors in counselling and in related disciplines. Subsequently in 1964, the KCA formed an ethics committee and began regulating the qualification and professionalism of school counsellors. The major incident that contributed to the professional growth of school counsellors during this period was the legislation of the Chief School Counselling System enacted in 1973, whereby the counselling system was installed in schools by law. Counselling centres and senior counsellors were provided for middle and high schools, offering classes and services that largely covered counselling, information dissemination, psychological test administration, research and investigation. Among the methods adopted for school counselling, Rogers's non-directive approach has been always predominantly used. Some of the behaviour modification methods and the training programme called 'mind development' were also used in the 1970s. Within this context, in 1978, developmental counselling was brought in by Lee Hyung-Deuk and Byun Chang-Jin who had studied in the United States. However, the training of school counsellors during this period was still unstructured and without competent professional trainers. Moreover, the roles of school counsellors were very ill-defined: little orientation was provided and they did not have a clear idea of their role as a counsellor at schools. In actuality, senior teachers after having taken two or three counselling courses to a total of about 360 hours could become counselling teachers. Most of them had poor understanding of the essentials of counselling and little knowledge of counselling skills, and were mostly perceived as disciplinarians rather than counsellors.

On the other hand, since the first counselling centre opened at the Seoul National University in 1962, many counselling centres were set up at colleges and universities throughout the country. They extensively provided individual and group therapy and career and academic guidance to the college student populations. Many of these counselling centres also played the role of counselling training centres, and had internship programmes in which beginning counsellors and graduate students practised their counselling skills and received supervision from more advanced counsellors. The 'Korean College Counsellors' Association (KCCA)' formed in 1974 committed itself to the establishment of professional counselling through workshops, seminars and trainings, introducing counselling theories and individual and group counselling programmes. Now more than 100 universities, including private universities, have their own counselling and guidance centres.

In 1985, the Seoul City Education Committee launched a programme entitled 'Voluntary Counselling Service for Students'. Under the scheme, school counselling volunteers were selected by the local counselling centres and given training in counselling theories and group counselling workshops. Then, they were appointed to schools counselling posts. The scheme had spread all over the nation by 1988. It certainly contributed to revitalise school counselling services and diffuse public recognition. In 1990, the Ministry of Education created the Department of Career Education under the Education Institute improving school-based career education and student counselling. In the same year, the 'Korea Youth Counselling Institute' started to present its own youth counselling theories and techniques. Programs such as peer group counselling, character development training, teacher training and parent training were introduced. Some schools incorporated youth counselling into traditional school counselling. During this time, counselling organisations and institutions specialising in issues related to women also started to provide sex education in schools, contributing to the development of more multi-faceted school counselling.

In 1997, the Elementary and Secondary School Education Act led to a training system for registered professional school counselling teachers. However, many registered school counselling teachers were not yet appointed as school counsellors. In 1999, the Ministry of Education introduced the school social worker system which has substantially expanded the realm of school counselling. The newly revised Elementary and Secondary School Education Act in 2004 finally made a greater impact on the school counselling as a profession. This Act prepared and distributed funds to local school boards and universities to improve school counselling services and also foster school counsellors. From 2005, the Ministry of Education, Science and Technology started to place full-time school counselling teachers as professional school counsellors in secondary schools. Up to 2006, over 24,000 registered school teachers and trainees were certified by the Ministry of Education and Human Resources Development as school counsellors. In 2007, about 350 school counsellors were placed in both public and private schools and in 2008, another 132 school counsellors were placed in public schools. However, many of them were not always appointed as school counsellors. Despite the desperate and genuine need for professionalised school counselling supports, the number of school counsellors appointed in full-time posts reached only 880 in 2012, and governmental support and funds are still far behind. School counsellors constantly battle to establish their own roles distinct from those of guidance teacher and enhance their professional identity on the ground even to this day.

The increase in psychological and behavioural problems of adolescents was clearly the major reason for initiating school counsellors. The major roles of school counsellors, thus, lay in detecting, responding and preventing issues that each student presents or may be facing alone. It is noteworthy that each student at different developmental stages displays specific needs. For instance, in primary schools, an important aspect to consider should be the development and implementation of school guidance. While adjustment is mostly a critical issue in middle school, relationship or career counselling are crucial in high schools. Therefore, considering the distinctive developmental needs, school counsellors should be able to change their priorities in roles and activities, from guidance teachers to help providers to relationship and career counsellors. School counsellors are evidently required to develop the ability to prioritise roles and activities to respond sensitively to unique needs at diverse stages of students' development. In recent years, academic pressure has been a lethal cause for the psychological

Figure 6.2 D-middle school, mid-term exam © 2009 Samuel Orchard: according to the Korean Statistical Information Service (KOSIS), the suicide rate of 8.9 per cent per 100,000 population was observed in the age group of 15–19 (in 2011). 39.2 per cent of respondents identified the stress about school records or exams as major causes of the impulse to commit suicide (in 2012)

and behavioural breakdowns of many students in middle and high school and even children in primary schools. School counsellors' roles have now extended to providing counselling for more serious societal and mental issues of group bullying and suicide attempts. The need for a professional counselling system and competent school counsellors grows more serious.

Pastoral counselling

Since the arrival of Protestant missionaries in 1884, Protestantism has rapidly grown to become the biggest religion in Korea after Buddhism. The total number of Catholics and Protestants is larger than that of Buddhists. Especially after the Korean War in the early 1950s, Korea was reinforced by the influx of strong Christian influences brought by Western missionaries and Korean-based US servicemen. Since the early 1960s, the number of Protestants has increased faster with an average of 10 per cent each year. More than 58,600 churches and over 95,590 pastors were reported by 2008. Although the number of Protestants has been decreasing since the mid-1990s, Korean churches always have a strong voice in Korean society as leading authorities. These Christian churches, under the strong influence of Western Christianity, have played a major part in the propagation of Western values and lifestyle in Korean society. In the same way, Korean Christians have been highly receptive to the Western mode of contemporary pastoral care and counselling, particularly in academic contexts.

Rev. Lee Whan-Shin 이환신 (1902–1984) studied pastoral counselling at the University of Southern California and the Claremont Theological Seminary for two years. In 1951, he returned to Korea with numerous books on pastoral counselling and also translated *Psychoanalysis and Religion* by Erich Fromm. On

Figure 6.3 Lee Whan-Shin

resuming his teaching post at the Yonhui College (predecessor of Yonsei University), he offered a course entitled 'Question and Answer of Pastoral Ministry 문의학' which was the first pastoral counselling course to be taught in Korea. In 1960, he translated Caroll Wise's *Pastoral Counselling* (1951). In 1958, Rev. Han Sung-Ho 한성호 also returned to Korea after studying pastoral counselling at the Boston University and lectured at Methodist Seminary and the Ewha Woman's University. In 1963, he translated Carl Rogers's *Counselling and Psychotherapy* (1942). These early publications raised some awareness of the importance of counselling in Christian ministries and interests in pastoral counselling. However, trained teachers and reference materials were few and in particular clinical training was totally absent around this time. In 1970, the first Korean book on pastoral counselling, *Preface to Pastoral Counselling* was published by Hwang Ui-Young.

It was in 1974 when Rev. Peter van Lierop (also known by his Korean name Ban Pi-Deuk 반피득, 1918–2012) instituted a clinical programme at the Severance Hospital that the first clinical pastoral counselling eventually began in Korea. A missionary from the United States, who previously founded the Student Counselling Centre in 1968, Rev. Ban Pi-Deuk also opened the first course of clinical pastoral education at the Yonhui College in the same year. Essentially, he provided a foundation for learning both theories and practices of pastoral counselling. On the return of many Koreans with foreign educations in the 1970s and 1980s, some professional institutions emerged accelerating its further growth. During this time, the Tyrannus Ministry's Counselling School established in 1981 was one of the leading private institutions. With the abundant financial and personnel resources of the Onnuri Church opened in the 1980s, the School was significantly able to contribute to popularising and extending the importance of Christian counselling. Further, the Family Counselling Institute of the Tyrannus Ministry was set up in 1982, where psychiatric medical principles rather than biblical counselling were preferred as an approach. More importantly, the 'Korean Association of Pastoral Counsellors (KAPC) 한국 목회상담 협회' was established in 1982 providing a base for the development of pastoral counselling. The KAPC held the Asia Pacific Congress on Pastoral Care and Counselling in 1997 in Seoul and began providing the Pastoral Counselling Certificates since 1999.

The greater impetus to pastoral counselling began in the early 1990s when those who had been trained in the AAPC (American Association of Pastoral Counselling) model of pastoral counselling in the United States increasingly appeared in the field of pastoral counselling. They effected the development of the contemporary pastoral care and counselling movement in Korea. During this period, a number of professional associations were organised. The 'Korean Association of Biblical Counselling 한국 성경적상담 협회' was launched by Chung Chung-Sook in 1995. The 'Korean Society for Pastoral Care and Counselling 목회상담 학회' was set up in 1997 publishing the journal *Pastoral Care and Counselling*. In 1999, the 'Korean Association of Christian Counselling and Psychotherapy 한국 기독교상담 심리치료 학회' was organised by Lee Man-Hong together with Christian social workers, psychiatrists and scholars. The *Journal of Korean Christian Counselling and*

Psychotherapy played an important part in improving the academic standards of Korean Christian counselling by promoting academic researches and stimulating discussions for more comprehensive Christian counselling.

Other establishments at this time included the 'Korea Association of Spirituality and Psychotherapy 한국 영성 및 심리치료 협회 (2000)' and the 'Korea Evangelical Theological Society 한국 복음주의 기독교상담 학회 (2000)'. In 2001, the 'Korean Association of Clinical Pastoral Education' was established. Some hospitals, such as the Severance, the Korea University Hospital and the Chungnam University Hospital, became interested in pastoral care and adopted clinical pastoral education within hospital programmes. In the 2000s, many pastoral counselling centres – academy-based, independent or church-related – were established and many theological schools launched programmes related with pastoral counselling. Competition between different associations and institutions accelerated the active production of clinical articles and materials, strengthening their professional identity and professionalism different from general counselling. Nevertheless, exchanges and interactions between these associations or societies were relatively lacking as each wanted to maintain their vested interest, inevitably hindering from its greater development.

The representative figures for contemporary pastoral counselling include Oh Seong-Chun 오성춘 who presided over the 'Korean Association of Pastoral Counsellors (KAPC)' between 1998 and 2002 and that published numerous books and articles. Chung Tai-Ki 정태기, who established the 'Christian Healing and Counselling Institute' in 1996, providing counselling and training, strove to promote the 'Christian inner healing counselling 치유상담'. On the other hand, Lee Jae-Hoon 이재훈 after having majored in theology, went to the United States and studied counselling psychology and 'psychoanalysis and religion' in the early 1980s. Since then, his principal work has been spirituality and psychoanalysis. In 1996, he founded the 'Object Relations Institute for Psychoanalysis in Seoul' and introduced many books on object relations theory through translation. He headed the KAPC between 2002 and 2004.

Indeed, Korean pastoral counselling achieved outstanding achievements, considering its short history, in parallel with the rapid development of Korean economics and churches. Within the social ambiance, overwhelmed by the overall quantitative expansions, many Koreans sought pastoral care and counselling. The strong financial capacity of Korean churches was a contributing factor to development of numerous counselling centres, thereby the exceptional growth of the profession. Recently, many pastoral counsellors have begun to raise their voices to urge a systematic training and research and above all, mutual collaboration so as to prolong the continual development of pastoral counselling in Korea.

Note

1 Unlike in the United States where the terms counsellor and counselling psychologist refer to different credentials, in Korea they are used interchangeably.

Bibliography

Chung, C. S. (2003). A historical examination of Christian counselling education in Korea. *Chongshin Review*, 8, 5–30.

Huh, S.H., & Park, S. M. (2005). The need analysis of parents, teachers and school administrators about elementary school counsellor roles and functions. *Journal of Elementary Education*, 18 (1), 19–38. [Korean]

Joo, E. S. (2009). Counselors in South Korea: a qualitative study of senior professionals. *Journal of Counselling and Development*,87 (4), 466–475.

Keum, M. J. (2007). Differences between expected and anticipated roles of the school counselors. *Korean Journal of Counselling and Psychotherapy*, 19 (4), 843–861. [Korean]

Kim, A. E. (1995). A history of Christianity in Korea: From its troubled beginning to its contemporary success. *Korea Journal*, 35 (2), 39–53.

Lee, S. M., & Yang, E. J. (2008). School counselling in South Korea: Historical development, current status and prospect. *Asian Journal of Counselling*, 15 (2), 157–181.

Seo, Y. S., Kim, D. M., & Kim, D. I. (2007). Current status and prospects of Korean counselling psychology. *Applied Psychology An International Review*, 56 (1), 107–118.

Seol, K. M., & Lee, H. D. (1993). Developmental Counselling Movement in Korea. In A. H. Othman & A. Awang (Ed.). *Counselling in the Asia-Pacific Region* (pp. 83–102). Westpost, CT: Greenwood.

You, Y. G. (2011). History and future of Korean pastoral counselling. *The e-Journal of the American Association of Pastoral Counselling*, 3, 120– 135. [Korean]

7 Implementation of Western psychotherapy

As early as the 1930s, the concept of Western psychotherapy was introduced into Korea, but it was in the 1950s after the Korean War (1950–1953) through the contacts with American military psychiatrists and psychologists that Korean clinicians actually became acquainted with the practice of psychotherapy. In the mid-1960s, several Korean psychiatrists who accomplished psychoanalytically-oriented training in the United States or Switzerland returned to Korea and became leading practitioners promoting dynamic psychiatry and psychoanalysis. A zest for psychoanalysis continued until the late 1960s when many of those foreign-trained psychiatrists started to find it difficult to adopt this approach with Korean patients, mostly because of the Koreans' cultural climate: inclination to simply enumerate problems; expectation of direct answers and specific guidance; and reluctance to talk at length about personal thoughts and feelings to a stranger. Since 1962 when Carl Rogers's work was introduced, person-centred therapy became almost instantly the primary method in practice and this lasted until the early 1980s. In the 1970s and the 1980s, with greater numbers of malaises resulting from the rapid development and transformation of Korean society, not only mental health experts but also the general public began to pay more attention to psychotherapy. Several professional psychotherapy organisations were established during this period. In the mid-1980s, cognitive behavioural therapy was introduced and has enjoy great popularity since the 1990s.

In the development of psychotherapy in Korea, the field has consisted of largely four main types of professional: psychiatrists; clinical psychologists; psychiatric social workers; and other mental health practitioners inclusive of counsellors, expressive therapists, family therapists and psychoanalysts. Among these practitioners, psychiatrists have had the strong political voice and professional jurisdiction over psychotherapeutic practices. Until 1996, psychiatrists were the only mental health professionals who were 'legally' allowed to practise psychotherapy in Korea. In 1997, the Mental Health Act was enforced and from 1998, the Ministry of Health and Welfare has issued licences to qualified mental health professionals in the areas of clinical psychology and psychiatric social work. This spurred the expansion of psychotherapy in Korea. These professionals primarily practise in hospital settings. Some clinical psychologists have begun working in private clinics or counselling centres alongside counsellors.

Since the late 1990s, mental health professionals from various disciplines began to emerge and were entitled to be psychotherapists independent of the exiting helping professionals. This facilitated a sustained growth of both number and types of psychotherapy. These psychotherapists, trained as psychodynamic, analytical, expressive arts, play, gestalt or family therapists, have become the most active and accessible of all mental health professionals, playing multiple roles and providing a variety of important services to diverse groups of people and organisations. Although their professional roles and boundaries are not always well defined and that psychiatrists still exert the greatest power in the field, this has not hindered an increasing number of people from turning to these practitioners for help. Even though there are no government licences for psychotherapists in Korea yet, certificates are granted by relevant professional psychotherapy associations. In practice, more psychotherapists tend to use an eclectic mix of Western-based theoretical orientations, including psychoanalytic, humanistic and cognitive behavioural approaches.

Psychoanalytic psychotherapy 정신분석 심리치료

Introductory period: 1920s–1940s

Under the Japanese occupation in the early 1920s, the concepts of Freud's psychoanalysis were introduced through the Japanese psychiatrists. '*Keum-byung-dong* Book Catalogue 금병동 도서목록 of 1930–1939', published by the National Institute of Korean History in 2008, reveals that there was a 'Collection of Freud's Works' in Japanese translation[1] but was lost during the Korean War. A survey of the Korean History Electronic Database also produces, albeit in a very scattered and episodic manner, evidence of the introduction of psychoanalysis to Korea in Korean magazines and newspapers during this period. The magazine *Donggwang* 동광 in its eleventh issue dated 5 March 1927 printed an editorial article entitled 'Advocate of Sexual Education' by Kim Youn-Kyung, in which the term psychoanalysis and Freud were mentioned referring to the notion of sexual drive.

Dong-A daily newspaper 동아일보 also published the first article mentioning Freud in its issue printed on 14 October 1928. During the 1930s, it introduced several articles on Freud including a special article of 'Psychoanalysis, Authority, Freud' printed in its issue of 4 August 1938. Ahn Jong-Il 안종일, a psychiatrist trained in the Kyungseong Imperial College of Medicine wrote the medical columns in *Dong-A* daily newspaper between September 1932 and July 1936. In his column dated 4 March 1934, he mentioned that '*in treating sexual neurasthenia in particular, psychoanalysis was very effective*' referring to his own attempts at psychoanalytic therapy in practice as early as in 1929. He wrote two consecutive articles entitled 'Psychoanalytic Therapy for Suicidal People' on 11 and 12 October 1935. In these articles, Ahn Jong-Il explained the causes of suicidal ideas and the prevention of suicide through psychoanalytical therapy. A few articles introducing Jung, Adler and their theories also appeared during this period in *Dong-A* daily newspaper. There are some indications that the library of the Department of Neuropsychiatry of Kyungseong Imperial College of Medicine owned the original book of Carl G. Jung and his papers presented at the International Association of Psychiatrists but more detailed information remains unknown.

In the thirtieth issue of a magazine *Byeol-geon-gon* 별건곤 (別乾坤) published on 1 July 1930, a disciple of Morita Shoma (森田 正馬), Lee Ryong-Shick 이룡식 who belonged to the 'Medical Psychology Study Group 의삭심리 연구회' wrote on 'The Effects of Psychotherapy on Psychotic Patients' and presented the case of a 22-year-old woman he had treated: the woman suffered from physical symptoms of palpitation, headache and lethargy after an incident whereby a young man suddenly appeared when she was walking late at night. In short, her subconscious fear of a bad boy and the anticipatory fear were discussed, and her symptoms disappeared. This is regarded as the first detailed record of a Korean case study treated with the psychoanalytic method.

Establishment period: 1950s–1970s

The first Korean who was formally trained in psychoanalysis was Kim Sung-Hi 김성희 (1917–2003). He was first acquainted with Freud's psychoanalysis in the book *Interpretation of Dreams* when he was a medical student in Pyongyang. He was so impressed by the book that he decided to study psychoanalysis. In April 1940, he left for Tokyo and was introduced to Kosawa Heisaku 古澤 平作 (1897–1968). Kosawa, who had met Freud in Vienna, was one of the founding members of the Japanese Psychoanalytic Society together with Marui Kiyoyasu 丸井 清泰 (1886–1953). Kosawa introduced Kim Sung-Hi to Marui who had been one of the students of Adolf Meyer and was teaching then at the Sendai Imperial University. While having psychiatric training under the supervision of Marui at the Sendai Imperial University Hospital, Kim Sung-Hi had a personal analysis with him, 60 minutes a session on couch, six times a week. At the same time, he had didactic training of psychoanalytic theory with Kosawa every week for four years travelling back and forth to Tokyo.

Kim Sung-Hi appreciated Freud's paper 'Recommendations to Physicians Practicing Psychoanalysis' (1912) the most and translated it into Korean. Firmly insisting that only the rule of free association should be applied, Kim Sung-Hi adhered to the free association based on Freud's topographical model, while assuming a critical attitude to the analysts' interpretation and Freud's structural theory which might confine human mind to a narrow frame of theory by trying to analyse a phenomenon. During the Second World War, Kim Sung-Hi returned to Pyongyang in North Korea and practised psychoanalysis in this city which had fallen by then under the communist regime. Considered to be the first Korean psychoanalyst, Kim Sung-Hi was, however, tortured because of his practice of psychoanalysis under the communist regime that did not allow any practise of mind-related works including religions and psychoanalysis. He escaped to South Korea during the Korean War. Within the social chaos caused by the war and political revolutions, unfortunately, he was unable to have any contact with international psychoanalytic associations during this period. In 1952, he moved to Gwangju in the southern part of Korea to set up the Department of Psychiatry in the Chonnam National University Medical School where he taught and practised psychoanalysis sincerely for 24 years. In 1975, Kim Sung-Hi published a remarkable paper entitled 'Psychotherapy and Understanding of Schizophrenic Delusion' in which he explained how he treated a schizophrenic patient using neither medication nor electric shock treatment, but only by talking. Consequently, he then set a counterargument against Freud who claimed that schizophrenics could not be analysed because a schizophrenic would develop no transference.

The Korean War provided some crucial opportunities, notably for Korean psychiatrists who encountered American dynamic psychiatry through American military psychiatrists, to go to the United States in order to gain psychoanalytic training after they were discharged from the army service. During this time, they were exposed to both Freudians and Neo-Freudians – those from the schools of Karen Horney, Erich Fromm and Harry S. Sullivan. When they returned, they propagated what they had leant and experienced with enthusiasm, and played the pivotal role in offering psychoanalytic training which became one of the major areas of study in psychiatric training. One of them was Rhee Dong-Shick 이동식 who in later years developed Taopsychotherapy by integrating the practice of *Tao* into the psychotherapeutic practice. He went to the United States with a recommendation from an American military psychiatrist to study psychoanalysis. In 1953, Rhee Dong-Shick presented a clinical case in which he successfully treated a patient of psychogenic headache after 12 sessions of psychotherapy. This case was reported in a medical journal in 1960: a 25-year-old medical student complained of a headache for which no medication was effective for two years before the patient came to consult him. The reason for his headache was not apparent. Rhee Dong-Shick asked the patient to tell him everything that arose in his mind. It was then discovered that the patient started to have a headache after three months of blaming himself for being 'bad and guilty' as he was feeling jealousy and hatred towards a classmate excelling him in their studies. Prior to this, he had lost a brother and a sister who had given him emotional support. His father was extremely severe with him and urged him to be 'always good' with others. Talking of his father during the sessions, he realised how he had developed the tendency of feeling obliged to remain 'always good' to others. As the realisation took place, the headache went away. This is regarded as the first reported successful case of psychodynamic psychotherapy in Korea.

On 6 May 1957, the 'Symposium on Psychoanalysis in Commemoration of Sigmund Freud's 101st Birthday' was held in the Grand Auditorium at the Seoul National University of Medicine by the 'Korean Neuropsychiatric Association 대한신경정신 학회' (est. 1945), under the leadership of Myung Ju-Wan. It attracted an audience of over 2,500 people. Thirteen papers were presented at this symposium. The list of topics included: 'major conceptions of Freudian psychoanalysis'; 'the development of psychoanalysis'; 'Freud's theory of hysteria'; 'libido and sexual instincts theory'; 'Freud's theory of dream analysis'; 'Freud and wit'; 'psychoanalysis and art'; 'psychoanalysis and group psychology'; 'psychoanalysis and religion'; 'philosophical background of psychoanalysis'; 'critique of sexual instincts theory'; 'Neo-Freudian Karen Horney'; 'Freud in contemporary American psychiatry'.

Among those who were exposed to psychoanalysis during this period, there were notably Yu Seok-Jin, Jin Sung-Gi and Choi Shin-Hae. Yu Seok-Jin 유석진, one of the early major figures in Korean psychiatry, was sincerely committed to reading and teaching psychoanalytic literature. With other junior psychiatrists, he translated some of Freud's works into Korean. Unfortunately, these disappeared during the Korean War before their publication. Choi Shin-Hae 최신해 who opened the first psychiatry hospital Chungryangri-Nwoe in 1945 focused on couple psychoanalysis. Jin Sung-Gi 진성기who published an article entitled 'A Psycho-analytical Study of Korean Myth' in 1957 in the Korean *Journal of Neuropsychiatric Association* studied the Korean myth in the light of psychoanalysis.

In 1961, *The Interpretation of Dreams* was translated into Korean by Lee Yong-Ho 이용호. Since the late 1960s, those psychiatrists who were trained abroad began returning home and taught and practised psychotherapy. In 1968, Jung's analytical psychology was introduced by Rhi Bou-Yong. Later in 1969, Hahn Dong-Se 한동세, the first Korean psychiatrist who was certified by the American Board of Psychiatry and Neurology, published the first textbook of Korean 'Psychiatry 정신과학' for medical students, doctors and other scholars working with mental issues. This book contained many psychoanalytic and psychotherapeutic ideas in addition to case examples. It contributed to rapidly bringing Freud's ideas to the attention of Korean psychiatrists. Hahn Dong-Se also introduced psychodrama literature for the first time into Korea. Psychodrama was adopted by some hospitals in the 1970s.

Expansion period: 1980s–

In the 1980s, the new historical era of Korean psychoanalytic psychotherapy began with the respective development of both Jungian analytical psychology and Freudian psychoanalysis in parallel. Each group has been actively diffusing psychoanalytic practices since their beginnings. In addition, the 'Lacanian Study Group' was organised in 1992 by Kim Jong-Ju. In 1998, the group grew into the 'Korean Society for Lacan and Contemporary Psychoanalysis' and started publishing the *Journal of Lacan and Contemporary Psychoanalysis*. However, in Korea, Lacanian psychoanalysis has appealed more to scholars with philosophical or literary interests than to practitioners of psychoanalysis.

Jungian analytical psychology

Rhi Bou-Yong, a graduate from the C. G. Jung Institute in Zürich, returned to Korea in 1968 and began to promote the ideas of Jung and Analytical Psychology at the Department of Psychiatry in the Seoul National University College of Medicine, where he lectured and worked as a professor of psychiatry and psychotherapy. Despite the ambience of Korean psychiatry that has been mostly exposed and oriented to Freudian psychoanalysis, some young psychiatrists became very enthusiastic. It was the beginning of a new adventure in Jungian psychology in Korea. It was particularly warmly welcomed by some theologians, scholars of Buddhism and literature.

In 1978, as Lee Zuk-Nae, the second Korean Jungian analyst returned home, Rhi Bou-Yong organised with him and young analysands the 'Study Group for Analytical Psychology 분석심리학 연구회', then later 'Korean Society for Analytical Psychology (KSAP) 한국 분석심리 학회'. Since then, they have made constant efforts to spread Jung's spirit through regular academic meetings, case presentations, conferences and symposiums. They have also published several books on analytic psychology. Han Oh-Su joined in 1984 after six years of studying at the C. G. Jung Institute Zürich, followed by Lee Chul who also studied in Zürich. In 1983 in commemoration of the hundredth anniversary of the birth of C. G. Jung, a photo-exhibition with film and lectures on C. G. Jung and analytical psychology was held in Seoul and Daegu, sponsored by the Swiss Cultural Foundation. Finding great resonance among the Korean public, it marked a new era in analytical psychology development in Korea. The members of the KSAP are mostly psychiatrists and psychologists, and others are scholars in related fields. They meet on a regular basis and once a year have a national meeting to present formal papers. The first development of a training schedule for Jungian analysts and the publication of the official journal of the Society, 'Shim-Song Yon-Gu 심성연구 (*Study of Mind*)' in 1986 is noteworthy. Many of Jung's books have been also translated into Korean.

When the International Analytical Psychology Pilot Programme was inaugurated in 1996 by The C. G. Jung Institute of San Francisco, Suh Dong-Hyuck was selected as a first foreign scholar. Frequent contact with San Francisco Jungians and Jungians from the institutes of New York, Zürich and Tokyo has been established. Rhi Bou-Yong has also been personally in contact with Jungians abroad, particularly in Switzerland, the United States and Japan. Upon retiring from the Seoul National University College of Medicine in 1997, Rhi Bou-Yong founded with his Jungian colleagues the 'C. G. Jung Institute of Korea 한국 융 연구원' in order to focus more on the training of Jungian analysts. In 2003, Korean Jungian analysts with their base at the C. G. Jung Institute of Korea organised the 'Korean Association of Jungian Analysts (KAJA) 한국 융분석가 협회'. In 2007, the KAJA became a training group of the International Association of Analytical Psychology (IAAP). In 2013, there were 21 Jungian analysts in Korea who are IAAP members and 30 trainees from diverse academic backgrounds such as philosophy, theology, or education, as well as psychiatry and psychology. The C. G. Jung Institute of Korea, as the training and research centre of analytical psychology, has published the Korean translation of nine complete volumes[2] of C. G. Jung's 'Grundwerke (Basic Works; 기본 저작집)' by Walter Verlag between

2001 and 2008. The Institute also published the first volume of the *Studies of Analytical Psychology from C. G. Jung Institute of Korea* in 2012.

Rhi Bou-Yong 이부영

Rhi Bou-Yong (1932–) travelled to Zürich in 1962 during his psychiatry residency training at the Seoul National University Hospital to study at the C. G. Jung Institute Zürich, where he was analysed by Franz Riklin and then by Marie-Louise von Franz. In 1966, he graduated from the Institute with a thesis on Korean Shamanism that he had enthusiastically written from a newly obtained Jungian symbolic perspective. In the winter semester of the Institute in 1966–1967, he gave a lecture on the 'Psychology of Shamanism'. In summer 1971, he gave another lecture on the 'Concepts of Illness and Healing in Korean Shamanism'. In 1968, he returned to Korea and became joined the faculty of Department of Psychiatry in the Seoul National University College of Medicine. Since then, he has been fully committed to teaching Jungian psychology to trainees, professionals and to the general public.

As the founder of 'Korean Analytical Psychology', Rhi Bou-Yong's primary concern was whether Jungian analysis was useful for Koreans and how well it worked. At the beginning, he recognised some culturally determined elements in administering the analytic process. He presented his observations under the title 'Analysis in Korea with Special Reference to Success and Failure in Analysis' on the occasion of the IAAP Congress in London in 1971. From his further investigations and experiences in Jungian psychotherapy in Korea, he became convinced that Jungian psychotherapy could be successfully applied to Koreans only if one takes cultural factors into consideration. Since then, he has extensively

Figure 7.1 Rhi Bou-Yong

investigated and written about Korean Shamanism, myth, folklore and traditional thoughts in Buddhism, Taoism, Neo-Confucianism and encouraged Korean Jungians to pursue further researches into a verification of Jungian psychotherapy in Korean culture.

Starting with the textbook, '*Analytical Psychology: C. G. Jung's thoughts of mind* 분석심리학: C. G, Jung의 인간 심성론' (1978), he then wrote and translated many books of and on Jung, offering them as a guide for the public to the basic approach of C. G. Jung towards the human mind. He published a book *The Depth Analysis of the Korean Folktale* in 1995 and numerous articles on Korean folklore and traditional Eastern thoughts from the perspective of Jungian analytical psychology. In 1995, he taught at the Union Theological Seminary in New York as a visiting professor. Upon his retirement from the Seoul National University College of Medicine in 1997 after a distinguished career as a leading psychiatrist and Jungian analyst, having received many national and international awards, Rhi Bou-Yong founded the 'C.G. Jung Institute of Korea' and continues to reinforce the foundations of analytical psychology in Korea. His most recent publications in addition to three volumes of *The Studies in Analytical Psychology* (1999–2002) are: *The Korean Shamanism and Analytical Psychology: toward the symbols of the suffering and the healing* (2012) and *Lao-tzu and C. G. Jung: a Jungian interpretation of Lao Zi Dao De Jing* (2012).

Lee Zuk-Nae 이죽내

Lee Zuk-Nae (1940–) became the second Korean Jungian who went to study at the C. G. Jung Institute Zürich in the 1960s and graduated in 1978. He returned home and joined in the activities of the 'Korean Study Group for Jung's Analytical Psychology' organised by Rhi Bou-Yong. At the same time, he taught and practised at the Department of Psychiatry in Kyungbuk University School of Medicine, devoting himself to the training of Jungian psychotherapy for young psychiatrists. In the meantime, he frequently visited Zürich to undergo a second training analysis in 'Daseinanalysis 현존재분석', the existential analytical school of Medard Boss and became the first Korean Daseinanalyst. He translated *Psychoanalysis and Daseinsanalysis* of Medard Boss into Korean. Furthermore, as a great scholar on traditional Eastern philosophies and Buddhist psychotherapy, Lee Zuk-Nae published *Jungian Psychology and Eastern Thoughts* and many articles on analytical psychology and Korean traditional culture and thoughts and has been invited to many conferences on Buddhism and Psychotherapy. He is also an active member of the executive committee and the training analyst of C. G. Jung Institute of Korea.

Han Oh-Su 한오수

Han Oh-Su (1945–), the third Jungian analyst in Korea, studied psychiatry at the Seoul National University College of Medicine. During his psychiatry residency

Figure 7.2 Lee Zuk-Nae

training at the Department of Neuropsychiatry in the Seoul National University Hospital, he began studying analytical psychology and regularly took Jungian analysis. He was involved in the academic activities of the Study Group for Analytical Psychology since its foundation. Upon the completion of his psychiatry specialist training, in 1978 he went to study at the C. G. Jung Institute Zürich. In 1984, he returned home and took part in activities of the KSAP undertaking the reading of the German texts of Jung. While practising as a Jungian psychotherapist, he worked at the Seoul Chung-Ang Hospital and the Ulsan University Medical School, teaching young psychiatrists analytical psychotherapy until his retirement in 2010. As one of the founding members of the C. G. Jung Institute of Korea, Han Oh-Su has been actively involved in training and supervising analysts of the Institute, as well as research. Currently, he leads the translation committee of the Institute responsible for the Korean translation of the Works of Marie Louise von Franz. His other major interests are the Korean founding myth of Dan Gun, religious experiences of the mystics and Jung's Red Book. He has been a registered member of IAAP since 1995.

Freudian psychoanalysis

On 6 May 1980 in commemoration of Freud's birthday, the 'Seoul Psychoanalytic Study Group' was initiated under the leadership of Cho Doo-Young. It consisted of five other psychiatrists: Oh Seung-Hwan, Kim Eyong, Kim Hyun-Woo, Han Dong-Soo and Sohn Jin-Wook. This group was later renamed (in 1989) the 'Korean Association of Psychoanalysis (KAPA) 한국 정신분석 학회'. The organisation of the group was not gladly accepted. Both the previously established Jungian group and the psychotherapy group had been running respectively the study groups of psychoanalytic orientated study, and were a little wary of another new group. Despite the lukewarm reception that challenged those who were enthusiastic about Freudian psychoanalysis, the group progressively grew, holding biweekly bookreading seminars on Wednesday evenings. In 1985, some of the KAPA members attended for the first time the Congress of the International Psychoanalytical Association (IPA) founded by Sigmund Freud. Since then, the KAPA has regularly attended the IPA Congress and readily cooperated with the IPA. This resulted in the KAPA being accepted into the IPA as its first Guest Study Group at the occasion of the IPA Congress in Buenos Aires in 1991. Domestically, the Korean Academy of Medical Sciences granted the KAPA a regular membership as representative of the psychoanalytic sector in Korea.

Since 1990, the KAPA has published the journal *Psychoanalysis*, the only journal of Freudian psychoanalysis in Korea. It is currently published biannually. In 2000, the KAPA started the first two-year programme of 'Advanced Psychoanalytic Psychotherapy Training'. This course is restricted to psychiatrists and approximately ten psychiatrists participate in the course every year. In 2009, the KAPA launched the four-year 'Psychoanalytic Training Program', as yet closed to non-medical candidates. At the forty-third IPA Congress in 2004, Jeong Do-Un and Hong Tak-Yoo were approved as direct members of the IPA. Shortly after, Yu Jae-Hak, Kim Mee-Kyung and Lee Moo-Suk were also qualified as direct members of the IPA. As having five direct IPA members in 2008, the KAPA's guest study group was upgraded to a formal study group of the IPA. In 2013, Chung Sun-Ju became another new member of the IPA.

Cho Doo-Young 조두영

Cho Doo-Young (1937–) studied psychiatry at the Seoul National University and went to the Cornell University Medical Centre in the United States for the psychiatry residency programme in the late 1960s. He had the experience of being in personal analysis for two years during his stay in New York. Since his return to Korea in the 1970s, he has devoted himself to the development of psychoanalysis and psychotherapy in Korea, making a significant contribution. In his role as a medical school faculty member at the Seoul National University College of Medicine between 1974 and 2002, he enthusiastically educated psychiatric residents and students on psychoanalysis and psychotherapy. In 2002, Cho Doo-Young received the Sigourney Trust Award for the first time in Asia, in recognition of his contribution to the development of psychoanalysis. He donated the award for use of further development of psychoanalysis in Korea.

Further developments

There has been much debate concerning the effectiveness of psychoanalysis in Korean patients, arguing that psychoanalysis is not appropriate for Koreans

Figure 7.3 Cho Doo-Young

mainly due to their lacking an insightful attitude and tendency to depend on therapists. Some have claimed that resistance commonly occurs when they are faced with the issues that call for insight into their inner conflict. Culturally speaking, Koreans who put emphasis on human relations of '*Jeong* 정' and particularly place heavy importance on non-verbal communication tend to expect others to know or understand what they want by means of their facial expressions or reading the situations using '*Noonchi* 눈치'. In the same way, Korean patients often expect the analyst to know what they are thinking without expressing their inner thoughts and feelings. Some have argued that these ways of communication cause difficulties in psychoanalysis.

On the other hand, Lee Moo-Suk 이무석 (1945–), a member of the International Psychoanalytical Association since 2007, argues that Koreans' non-verbal communication custom is of more help for an analysis as the communication in psychoanalysis is basically about the 'communication between the analyst and the child-within' often involving non-verbal communication. He also claims that through their marked family centeredness and collectivism, Korean patients easily establish a family-like relationship with the analyst on which the characteristics of transference depend. Hence, Lee Mu-Suk insists that Koreans have a rather well-suited cultural background for psychoanalysis. Nonetheless, evidence to support his arguments and prove positive effects of psychoanalysis for Korean patients are scarce at this point. Other Korean psychoanalysts, while believing in basic theories of psychoanalysis, suggest some technical modifications to be made to allow for the unique cultural differences of Koreans. Those who share these ideas go forward with Neo-Freudians or the integration of *Tao* practice.

Humanistic psychotherapy 인본주의 심리치료

The humanistic psychotherapy approach in Korea began with the humanist education movement in the late 1950s. It received attention by way of student guidance in accord with the then liberal democratic educational ideals and humanity development. During this period, guidance and counselling theories emphasising the personality and aptitude of individuals were taught as a basic course in youth guidance workshops organised for school teachers. In a questionnaire conducted in 2003 asking Korean psychotherapists what is the main theory or method they favour, 73.8 per cent of them reported that it is the humanistic approach. In its background, there is certainly similarity between humanistic psychotherapy and the Korean traditional cultural and ethical values ultimately placed in the humanity-centred consciousness. Although the number has fallen due to the popularity of cognitive behavioural therapy, humanistic psychotherapy remains the most preferred orientation of counsellors and counselling psychologists in Korea. Since the early 1970s, the two major movements are now found in approaches of Korean humanistic psychotherapy. One can be described as an 'oriental attempt' by psychiatrists and psychologists in the psychotherapy field invoking Buddhism and Taoism. Another is the integration of Eastern and Western theories and the search for a Korean model in educational and counselling psychology.

Person-centred therapy 인간중심 심리치료

Kim Sung-Hi 김성희 (1917–2003), who received an early exposure to Freud and psychoanalysis theories in the 1940s, is also considered to be the first mental health professional to apply the person-oriented approach before the introduction of the person-centred approach of Carl Rogers to Korea. In the atmosphere of strong prejudice against mental patients in the 1950s and the 1960s, Kim Sung-Hi, who established the Department of Psychiatry in the Chonnam National University Medical School in Gwangju in 1952, insisted on running the Hospital as an open ward despite strong opposition from colleagues. He was convinced that only an open ward system would offer a suitable therapeutic environment for the patients. Claiming that if one removed symptoms with drugs, one would also remove the motivation for treatment, Kim Sung-Hi was reluctant to give diagnoses and prescribe drugs. He was also fiercely against the use of electronic shock therapy which was prevalent at that time. Instead, he emphasised 'here-and-now' and empathetic understanding as a more efficient therapeutic method. During his tenure of practice until 1976, Kim Sung-Hi remained faithful to such approaches that were indeed very close to the methods of person-centred therapy.

From 1962, the theory of Carl Rogers was taught and researched among counselling psychologists at the Student Counselling Centre of Seoul National University and it became very popular with school counsellors. Since *Counselling and Psychotherapy* (1942) was first translated into Korean in 1963, many books of his have been translated. In the 1960s and the 1970s, person-centred therapy was the primary method in Korea until the advent of cognitive behavioural therapy. Lee Chang-Ho, who developed 'Integral Counselling 통합상담', assimilating an oriental mode of meditation and yoga, is the leading figure who has induced the development of the person-centred therapy. In 1980, he visited the 'Center for the Study of the Person at La Jolla' in California and met Carl Rogers. After participation in the Forth International Forum for Personal Centred Approach held in Netherlands in 1992, Lee Chang-Ho set up the 'Korean Person-Centred Approach Institute' in the same year. Later in 2007, he also launched the 'Korean Association of Rogerian Counselling (KARC) 한국 로저스상담 학회'. The KARC has since put special efforts into researching person-centred counselling theories to develop a person-centred approach that is appropriate in Korean culture.

Experts and their studies assert that the tenets of person-centred therapy like 'here and now', empathy and relatedness perfectly correspond to Korean culture and values. On the other hand, some have pointed out that the Rogerian approach does not guarantee solving problems and is too idealistic for Korean experiential realities. Nonetheless, in Korea, person-centred therapy remains a very familiar method in the field of counselling and psychotherapy.

Gestalt therapy 게슈탈트 심리치료

Gestalt therapy was initiated by Kim Jung-Kyu 김정규 (1951–). Kim Jung-Kyu was first exposed to gestalt therapy by attending a gestalt therapy group in 1986 in Bonn, Germany where he studied clinical psychology. After his return from Germany in 1988, he led a gestalt group of undergraduate students at the Sungshin Woman's University where he taught clinical psychology, abnormal psychology, gestalt therapy, group therapy and art therapy. In the following year, this group's membership was extended to the clinical and counselling psychology graduate students. Subsequently, he led a gestalt group for the general public both at the Korean Institute of Personal Development and at the Korean Mental Health Institute. Since 1994, he has run a Gestalt Leaders' Programme of three years' duration for psychologists and gestalt therapy trainees to train gestalt therapy experts. By 2013, 93 graduates were produced and more gestalt therapy professionals now work in various counselling centres. In collaboration with the 'Korean Gestalt Therapy Research Association 게슈탈트치료 연구회' that he founded in 2002 with over 200 affiliates, he has translated many gestalt therapy books into Korean. Since 2002, he has also been an editorial board member of the *International Gestalt Journal*. In 2010, Kim Jung-Kyu developed the 'Gestalt Relationship Improvement Program (GRIP)'. In the same year, the 'Korean Gestalt Therapy Association (KGTA) 한국 게슈탈트치료 학회' was inaugurated in the Sungshin Woman's University with the participation of 246 people. Kim Jung-Kyu became the first president of the organisation. The KGTA publishes its official journal, *The Korean Journal of Gestalt Therapy* twice a year and offers various training programmes, as well as supervision. It also issues a licence ensuring gestalt therapy practice. Today, gestalt therapy is well known in Korea and widely used as a framework for art, dance, drama and group therapies. Backed by the exceptional popularity of expressive art therapies, it is currently estimated that it is in Korea where gestalt therapy has most flourished in Asia.

In particular, Kim Jung-Kyu approaches gestalt therapy from the Buddhist perspective. He relates the concept of 'fertile void' mentioned by Fritz Perls to the Buddhist teaching of 'emptiness 공 (空)' or 'nothingness 무 (無)'. He observed the similarity in 'awareness' of gestalt therapy and 'mindfulness' of *vipassana*. Having been interested in integrating mindfulness meditation into gestalt therapy, Kim Jung-Kyu eventually developed, in 2001, a technique named 'PRO Meditation'. It consists of the three phases of 'Pause–Relax–Open 멈추고-풀고-열기'. Unlike existing meditation techniques, the PRO Meditation could be practised while in activity anywhere and at anytime. It is considered to be an effective method especially for people with anxiety disorder.

In addition to the aforementioned two approaches, existential therapy 실존심리치료 and philosophical therapy 철학심리치료 are practised in Korea. Existential therapy has been developed mainly through the efforts of professionals in theology and Christian psychotherapy. The 'Korean Existential Therapy Institute' opened by Lee Jung-Gi 이정기 who studied pastoral counselling in Chicago and now teaches at the Seoul Theological University has provided workshops since 2009. With its official opening in 2010, it has provided training, supervision and also certificates. Since 2007, philosophical therapy has been also active. In 2008, the 'Clinical Philosophy Society' was established and presided over by Kim Sung-Jin 김성진 who studied philosophy in Germany. Providing training focused

Figure 7.4 Gestalt therapy group workshop © November 2008 Author

on both Eastern and Western philosophies, it obtained official accreditation in 2011 and offers a certificate in philosophical therapy.

Cognitive behavioural therapy 인지행동 치료

In the mid-1980s, Lee Ho-Young, Won Ho-Taek and Kim Zoung-Soul made a great effort to introduce Cognitive Behavioural Therapy (CBT) in Korea. They trained psychiatric residents and graduate clinical psychology students in CBT. Gradually, the CBT group treatments for panic disorder, depression and social phobia were initiated in psychiatric hospitals. Their positive outcomes and efficiency stimulated further interest in CBT among clinicians. During this period, however, due to the training curriculum of psychiatrists in Korea, most psychotherapy training was limited to psychodynamic approaches, and only a few psychiatrists utilised CBT in their practice. Other mental health professionals who worked in hospitals – clinical psychologists, psychiatric nurses and social workers – needed to be supervised by a psychiatrist. As a result, CBT remained a minor form of therapy until the early 1990s when young clinical psychologists Chae Kyu-Man, Kwon Jung-Hye, Kwan Seok-Man and psychiatrists of a younger generation trained in the United States and came back to Korea with a commitment to practise and spread CBT. An important step was also taken by these young professionals as they translated and published the CBT textbooks and manuals into Korean. More young psychiatrists became impressed by this method and were eager to learn CBT, and many hospitals also began opening the CBT programmes. Moreover, clinical psychologists and other mental health professionals started to practise CBT outside of psychiatric hospitals. It served as an impetus to an enhancement of CBT in Korea.

In 1993, the 'Seoul Cognitive Therapy Counselling Centre 서울 인지치료 상담센터' was launched by two clinical psychologists, Kwon Jung-Hye 권정혜 and Min Byung-Bae 민병배. They treated their patients using CBT techniques without being supervised by a psychiatrist, which is still an obligation for psychologists working at hospitals. This marked a milestone in the history of Korean psychology for the first CBT treatments carried out by clinical psychologists independently of psychiatric settings. The success was definitely indebted to the enactment of the Mental Health Act in 1997, issuing licences for clinical psychologists to practise psychotherapy, as well as the increased interest of psychologists in clinical practices rather than carrying out psychological tests at the hospitals. The Centre was renamed 'Maumsarang Institute for Cognitive Behavioural Therapies' in 2007 and has been actively provided training, workshops and supervision.

The most exciting development in the dissemination of CBT in Korea was the emergence of a professional organisation, the 'Korean Association of Cognitive and Behaviour Therapy (KACBT) 한국 인지행동치료 학회'. Since its establishment in 2001, the KACBT has been organising numerous symposia, workshops and lectures for the wider audience of mental health professionals. The number of members in 2001 was less than 60 and has doubled in three years reaching over 350 in 2010, clearly indicating an increasing interest and acceptance of CBT in the field of psychotherapy. Its journal, *Cognitive Behaviour Therapy in Korea* biannually publishes original articles on application and implementation of CBT, serving as a major database of clinical experiences using CBT. In the past decade, the voice of a CBT approach that is more congruent to the beliefs and expectations of Korean patients has been raised. The CBT practitioners with this view explore the influence of Confucian principles, Buddhist teachings or other collective cultural heritage, which may provide a clue on the development of a CBT approach more appropriate for Koreans. Since the early 2000s, mindfulness meditation has also joined the mainstream of CBT in Korea.

Pioneers of cognitive behavioural therapy

Lee Ho-Young 이호영 (1932–), a psychiatrist, who had been working at John Runnells Hospital in New Jersey returned to Korea in 1984 and worked at the Yonsei University College of Medicine until 1990 and the Severance Hospital until 1994. In 1991, Lee Ho-Young launched the first CBT programme designed for panic disorders. At the time when the psychiatric hospitals still mostly focused on hospitalisation and medication for treatments, he introduced the 'Milieu Therapy 환경치료', a form of psychotherapy that combined the elements of therapeutic communities and practical activities with CBT group psychotherapy. Lee Ho-Young also introduced the 'Day Care' as a rehabilitation programme for chronic schizophrenic patients and successfully established it as a new treatment method in Korea.

Towards the end of the 1980s, many master and doctoral programmes in clinical psychology were set up and CBT was actively taught and researched, diverting the focus from the psychodynamic stance to the methods and researches of the cognitive behavioural approach. For example, more than two-thirds of 30 doctoral theses produced by the doctorates in clinical psychology between 1985 and 1996 reported studies on cognitive behavioural aspects of psychological disorders. Won Ho-Taek and Kim Zoung-Soul played the major role in training and supervising theses of young CBT practitioners. Won Ho-Taek 원호택 (1935–), a clinical psychologist who early on conducted psychotherapy at the hospital for the first time as a non-psychiatric doctor, attended the CBT workshop of Steven D. Hollon at Minnesota University in 1984, and extensively read Aaron Beck and Brian Shaw. Upon his return, he started practising CBT at the Seoul National University Counselling Centre. He conducted seminars and workshops on CBT for the clinical psychology research students at the Seoul National University. This served as a momentum to the increasing interest into research on CBT by Korean clinical psychologists. In particular, Won Ho-Taek and young professionals contributed to making another important step towards Korean CBT by publishing the Korean translation of *Cognitive Therapy of Depression* (by Aaron Beck, 1976) in 1996.

Kim Zoung-Soul 김중술 (1937–2013), who was trained in both psychology and psychiatry, was given the opportunity of an internship in clinical psychology at the Minnesota University between 1967 and 1968. After having taught at the Medical School of the Catholic University and the Suncheonhyang Hospital in Seoul, he moved to the Seoul National University College of Medicine in the early 1980s and set up, for the first time in Korea, a three-year internship programme in clinical psychology at the SNU Hospital, based on the internship model of the system of Minnesota University. While propagating the CBT techniques, he translated MMPI (Minnesota Multiphasic Personality Inventory) into Korean in 1988 and exerted himself to popularise it. His later interests and work involved more CBT marital counselling.

Expressive arts therapy 표현예술치료

When Western psychiatry was introduced to Korea, art activities were sporadically provided as a diversion in some psychiatric hospitals. They were mostly executed by non-experts such as psychiatrists, nurses, voluntary artists or art teachers. Yu Seok-Jin 유석진, a psychiatrist, first introduced the programme of 'art remedies 예술요법' in 1951. In the 1950s, he started offering music therapy debating how depression could be reduced after combining music therapy with medication. During the 1960s, Yu Seok-Jin continued to offer music therapy and implemented the programmes of music therapy in his St Peter's Neuropsychiatric Clinic, together with his wife Kim Myung-Hee 김명희 who studied music and had some training in music therapy in the United States. During this period, Jin Sung-Gi 진성기 also started music therapy at the Seoul National Hospital 국립 정신병원.

In the 1970s, more medical institutions, including the Seoul National Hospital (SNH) and the Seoul St Mary's Hospital 서울 성모병원 had art activities in their programmes, often led by social workers or nurses. During this period, some psychiatrists such as Lee Keun-Hu, Yu Seok-Jin and Kang Chun-Sang also started practising psychodrama, that had first been introduced through literature by Han Dong-Se in 1969. In 1973, Lee Keun-Hu 이근후 put on the four pieces of theatres, similar to psychodrama, in the psychiatric ward of the Ewha Woman's University Hospital; schizophrenic patients were given scenarios that were deliberately written in the way to help expose their inner minds, and objectify, explore and reconstruct them. In the following year, he published an article introducing 'psycho-theatre'. In 1975, Kim Yu-Kwang 김유광, a psychiatrist, conducted psychodrama at the SNH introducing the various theories. With this as a momentum, psychiatric hospitals started actively using psychodrama as a treatment method. In 1982, the 'Korean Art Remedies Research 한국 예술요법 연구회' that was renamed in 1983 'Korean Clinical Art Association 한국 임상예술 학회', was established by Yu Seok-Jin, Lee Keun-Hu and other like-minded psychiatrists. It was affiliated to the Korean Neuropsychiatric Association. This spurred the development of therapies through arts activities integrated with existing medical treatments within psychiatric wards.

Especially in the 1980s, prompted by the efforts of psychiatrist Choi Heon-Jin 최헌진, drama was presented as a therapeutic intervention at some universities. From the 1990s, it was extended to schools, workplaces and communities. With the inauguration of the 'Korean Association for Psychodrama and Socio-drama' in 1997, headed by Choi Heon-Jin, training and certificates that were previously limited to psychiatrists became gradually open to non-medical professionals; psychologists, educationalists and social-workers. In the late 1990s, drama therapy 연극치료 was developed as an independent field of therapy appealing to the general public. Han Myung-Hee 한명희 who was trained in the UK in the early 2000s, has been pioneering in the field of drama therapy in Korea. Subsequently, in 2005, Park Mi-Ri 박미리 founded the 'Korean Association of Drama Therapy' as a non-profit organisation affiliated to the Ministry of Culture, Sport and Tourism 문화관광부. This accelerated its prosperity. In the same year, the association opened a training course at the Sookmyung Woman's University. In recent years, drama therapy has been particularly successful as a guidance programme for teenage-related issues such as school violence or truancy.

In the 1980s, music therapy continued to progress. In 1981, Kim Kun-Ja 김군자 provided music therapy at the Ewha Woman's University speech-hearing clinical centre. Yu Seok-Jin, who had been actively involved in the promotion of music therapy, formed a music therapy research group in 1985 and started publishing its journal. In 1986, Yim Yeun-Hee 임은희, who studied music therapy in Canada, opened the first private clinic specialising in music therapy. Since then, many foreign-trained music therapists from the United States, Europe and Australia have embarked on similar work. Together, they have set up Korean music therapy programmes. Choi Byung-Cheol 최병철, who was trained in the United States in the late 1980s, launched the 'Korean Music Therapy Association 한국 음악치료 협회' in 1996. The following year, the graduate level of music therapy curriculum was initiated at the Sookmyung Woman's University where the educational and clinical training have become stronger. Currently, professional training courses and degree programmes of music therapy are provided by many other universities throughout the nation. They publish numerous clinical case studies and researches on music therapy.

In 1993, dance-movement therapy 무용-동작치료 was introduced at the Seoul National Hospital by Ryu Boon-Soon 류분순 who was trained in Germany. Since then, the 'Korean Dance-Movement Therapy Association' has been launched and 'techniques of dance therapy 무용요법' courses have been offered as a part of curricula in the dance departments of universities. Dance-movement therapy has achieved a small but sustained growth. On the other hand, art therapy 미술치료 started off by launching the master programme in 1991 at the Graduate School of Rehabilitation Science in the Daegu University under the leadership of Kim Dong-Yeon 김동연 (1947–2003). He established the 'Korean Art Therapy Association 한국 미술치료 학회' in the following year. Between 1998 and 2008, art therapy rapidly grew to include 10 graduate-level schools, 5

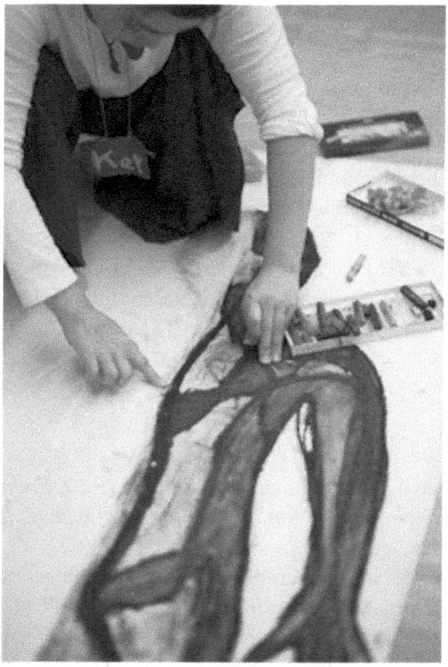

Figure 7.5 Art therapy workshop © September 2010 Author

undergraduate schools, 14 continuing education programmes, and 6 associations, ensuring art therapy as a firm profession. Since 2009, a doctoral programme has been offered. Moreover, the 'Korean Expressive Arts Psychotherapy Association (KEAPA) 한국 표현예술 협회' was founded in 1995 by Kim Jin-Sook 김진숙 who studied in New York and KEAPA has played a major role in implementing curricula in expressive arts psychotherapy at universities in their beginning, namely Dongguk University (1997) and Sookmyung Woman's University (1998).

Korean expressive arts therapy has been playing an important role since the late 1990s. Its development in Korea has been faster than for any of the other psychotherapy methods. Interest in the study of related therapies is continuously growing. Trained therapists work in educational, social and medical settings with a wide range of patient groups. In recent years, there have been more studies and research on developing expressive arts therapy approaches combined with Korean cultural assets – Korean traditional music, instruments, dances, stories and paints; for example, *samul-nori* (percussion music play), *tal-nori* (mask play), *sal-puri* (shamanic dance), *seol-hwa* (folktale) or *meok-hwa* (ink stick paints). Studies on Eastern art therapy approaches have been also investigated the possibilities for developing Eastern art therapy by combining it with Eastern thoughts.

Notes

1 Collection of Freud's works フロイド精神分析学全集 (1931). 分析藝術論 大槪憲二 春陽堂書店.

2 The Collected Works of Jung in 9 volumes: 1. Grundfragen zur Praxis (Basic Question about Practice) 정신요법의 실제 2. Archetyp und Unbewußtes (Archetype & Unconscious) 원형과 무의식 3. Persönlichkeit und Übertragung (Personality & Transference) 인격과 전이 4. Menschenbild und Gottesbild (Humanity & Godness) 인간의 상과 신의 상 5. Traumsymbole des Individuationsprozesses (Dream Symbols of Individuation) 꿈에 나타난 개성화광정의 상징 6. Erlösungsvorstellungen in der Alchemie (Salvation Ideas in Alchemy) 연금술에서 본 구원의 관념 7. Symbol und Libido (Symbol & Libido) 상징과 리비도 8. Heros und Mutterarchetyp (Heroes & Mother Archetype) 영웅과 어머니원형9. Mensch und Kultur (Man & Culture) 인간과 문화.

Bibliography

Jeong, D. U., & Sachs D. (2006). Psychoanalysis in Korea. In A. Salman (Ed.), *Freud and the Far East: Psychoanalytic Perspectives on the People and Culture of China, Japan, and Korea* (pp. 27–42). Plymouth: Jason Aronson.

Joo, E. S. (2011). International Trends in person-centered psychotherapy education and training. *Journal of Human Understanding and Counseling*, 32 (2), 1–22.

Joo, E. S., Bae, S., & Orlinsky, D. E. (2003). The professional and practice characteristics of Korean psychotherapists: Based on the 'International Study of the Development of Psychotherapists'. *Korean Journal of Counseling and Psychotherapy*, 15 (3), 423–440.

Kim, J. H. (2004). Types of mindfulness meditation and their implications for Cognitive Behavioural Therapy. *Cognitive Behaviour Therapy in Korea*, 4 (2), 27–44. [Korean]

Kim, K. I. (2000). Culture and psychoanalysis in Korea. *Journal of Korean Psychoanalytic Society*, 11 (2), 179–188.

Kim, S. H. (1975). Psychotherapy and understanding of schizophrenic delusion. *Chonnam Medical Journal*, 12, 699–711. [Korean]

Kim, Z. S. (2003). The Current Cognitive Behaviour Therapy and its problems in Korea. *Cognitive Behaviour Therapy in Korea*, 3 (1), 1–7.

Lee, C. H. (1995). Current status and problems of humanistic psychology in Korea. *SNU the Institute of Psychological Science*, 4 (1), 41–48. [Korean]

Lee, M. J. (2012). Understanding of Korean culture and values of art therapeutic approach. In D. L. Kalmanowitz, J. A. Potash, & S. M. Cha (Eds), *Art Therapy in Asia: To the bone or wrapped in silk* (pp. 102–114), London: Jessica Kingsley Publishers.

Lee, M. S. (2006). Life and works of professor Kim Sung-Hi. *Journal Korean Psychoanalytic Society*, 17 (1), 135–141. [Korean]

Lee, N. M., & Rhi, B. Y. (1999). The introduction of the Western psychiatry into Korea (1). *Korean Journal of Medical History*, 8 (2), 233–268.

Won, H. T. (2000). Four decades of clinical psychology in Korea. *Psychological Science*, 9 (1), 1–13.

8 Shaping of Korean psychotherapy

As a consequence of Western academics pouring into Korea, there has been a general tendency of blindly adhering to Western knowledge rather than pursuing a more prudent assimilation of newly acquired learning into existing traditional knowledge. This has been prevalent in Korean society as a whole. This phenomenon has no exception in the field of psychotherapy, and the tendency of recklessly following Western methods of psychotherapy without validating their suitability has taken place. Psychotherapy in Korea still excessively sticks to the concepts of Western psychotherapy and this misplaced attitude of assimilation within Korea continues to persist.

However, greater efforts to promote the integration of traditional Korean values and practices with the Western methods of psychotherapy have also been made in Korea, increasingly growing in recent years. One of the main attempts has been oriented to understanding Buddhist philosophy from the perspective of psychology and psychotherapy and acquiring the methods of meditation that can be used with Korean patients in a psychotherapy setting. Another distinguished accomplishment comes from Taopsychotherapy relating to the concepts of *Tao*.

Since 1965, a small group of dedicated Koreans, consisting of psychologists, psychiatrists, researchers and counsellors, has met regularly to study *Tao* 도 (道; way) and *Seon* 선 (禪 Zen; meditative state). Their common interest has been to understand how *Tao* and *Seon* have historically and culturally worked for the mental health of the Korean people and how they can be developed into therapeutic methods applicable in counselling situations. A leading member of the group, Rhee Dong-Shick who was a psychiatrist, took the lead and wrote extensively about the implication of *Tao* and *Seon* in psychotherapy and counselling. It was his contention that *Tao* and *Seon* provide an effective alternative of theory and technique for psychotherapy, given the general aim to achieve self-realisation and become one's own self. In the late 1970s, psychiatrists like Lee Keun-Hu and Lee Zuk-Nae made efforts to integrate Buddhist thoughts with counselling methods.

In the mid-1980s, the number of psychological research studies on the issues of applying Western psychotherapy with Korean patients multiplied. They mostly reported that Korean practitioners commonly experienced difficulties in applying a Western culturally-based theoretical orientation in a Korean setting, and thus

Figure 8.1 Kyungbong Sunim with Lee Keun-Hu, Rhee Dong-Shick, Yun Ho-Kyun (circled, from the left): Tongdo-sa, Yangsan © September 1974 The Korean Academy of Psychotherapists

turn to many different orientations at a time. Some academics and practitioners started taking the problems of such practice seriously and sought alternative paradigms for the identification of Korean psychotherapy. Since the 1990s, a growing number of Korean psychotherapists have been attempting to combine familiar notions of *Tao* and *Seon* in their practices to better attune to the needs of Korean people. They believe that *Tao* and *Seon* successfully teach an individual to identify and discard all biased preconceptions and beliefs caused either by the subjectivity of one's experience and cultural background, or the suppressed emotions such as hatred, guilt or anger, resulting in revealing the true inner self, thereby making the mind see the reality for what it is.

Taopsychotherapy

In the introductory period of Western psychotherapy when most Korean therapists were pessimistic about their practice, Rhee Dong-Shick, nonetheless, felt that Korean culture was very suitable for psychotherapy since it placed more emphasis on non-verbal emotional components and had a relationship orientation. Throughout the 1960s, one of his main concerns was the Korean inferiority complex which he believed, originated from historical defeatism, especially the experiences under Japanese imperialism. In an attempt to reach a better way for Korean people, in the mid-1960s, he started studying Korean history, culture and philosophy including Taoism, as well as Buddhism and Confucianism, with the support and teachings from prominent monks and scholars of each field. He believed that in order to help Korean people it was equitable to develop a psychotherapeutic approach drawn upon their own historical spiritual heritage. Soon, he realised how Western psychoanalysis and psychotherapies like Daseinsanalysis, existential analysis, person-centred therapy and transpersonal psychotherapy were all in fact, heading towards the notions of the *Tao*.

Hence, Taopsychotherapy – referred to as a 'profoundly humanistic, transpersonal, psychodynamic approach to psychotherapy' – was formulated around 1974 when he set up a weekly study group of psychotherapy cases. It was presented as a unifying practice modality intentionally aiming at fusing Western psychotherapy and psychoanalysis with Eastern traditional *Tao*. It takes a fundamentally humanistic approach offering a close analogue with Rogerian person-centred therapy. Like Daseinsanalysis following the hermeneutic ontology of Heidegger's *Daseinsanalytik*, Taopsychotherapy is equally an approach to understanding human existence and human suffering on philosophical and ontological grounds. Also, Taopsychotherapy aims at the same goal as transpersonal psychotherapy by trying to get the patient to transcend the self. In the view of Rhee Dong-Shick, all Western approaches to psychotherapy were reaching for the *Tao* and similarly the concepts of *unconscious, sein (being), empathy* were understood in the *Tao* philosophy. Both the *epoché* (suspension of judgement) in Husserl's phenomenology and *free association* and *evenly hovering attention* in psychoanalysis also correspond to the notions found in the *Tao*.

The essence of Taopsychotherapy

The essence of Taopsychotherapy is to reveal and overcome a patient's 'nuclear feeling' essentially through a therapist's deep compassion. To attain the absolute compassion, therapists need first to resolve their own nuclear feelings, thereby purify their mind. According to Rhee Dong-Shick, this purification of the minds corresponds to 'Non-doing' 무위 (無爲; Wu-wei) of Taoism, 'Emptiness' 공 (空; Sunyata) of Buddhism, 'No desire' of Confucianism and 'No-projection' (or no counter-transference) of psychoanalysis.

Nuclear feeling 핵심감정

Rhee Dong-Shick points out the primary importance of grasping and overcoming a patient's nuclear feeling which holds sway over his or her mind and behaviour throughout their life. According to him, these nuclear feelings are subjectively felt emotions cannot that be reached by intellectual pursuit or conceptual elaboration but by restless static contemplation which enables the therapist to constantly embody accurate compassionate responding. Akin to the various notions of Western psychoanalysis and psychotherapy such as complex, central dynamics, salient emotional pattern, major motivation, repetition, compulsion and so on, it is basically a central affect driven dynamic that lies at the core of a patient's most convoluted, intractable difficulties in life. Whereas those Western notions are conceptually formulated by the therapist's objective observation, comprehension and explanation, the nuclear feelings are fundamentally experiential and perceived through a therapist's complete compassion and mature personality. To obtain a complete compassion, and help a patient to remove his or her nuclear feelings, it is essential for therapists to remove first their own nuclear feelings. By completely removing the neurotic desires, i.e., nuclear feelings, Taopsychotherapy attempts to remove not only neurotic anxiety but existential anxiety originating from the fear of death.

Compassion

The therapist helps a patient realise and resolve the nuclear feelings essentially through therapeutic communication in a totally empathic way. One of the most important considerations in Taopsychotherapy is to be fully compassionate with a patient's feelings so that one can come to fully understand one's own feelings. In Taopsychotherapy, the practice and embodiment of compassion link directly with differentiated wisdom derived from the therapists' maturity achieved by resolving their own nuclear feelings and purifying their minds. It is related to the absolute liberation from the dichotomous way of viewing. Compassion is equivalent to empathy described as one of the necessary and sufficient facilitative core conditions for therapeutic change by Carl Rogers. Nonetheless, compassion that Rhee Dong-Shick is referring to, completely discounts the cognitive aspects of empathy. In this regard, Taopsychotherapy takes the viewpoint that the therapist's interpretation practically represents a lack of compassion in the therapist. In Taopsychotherapy, considerable emphasis is placed upon the maturity of the therapist, which enables him or her to attain absolute compassion with the patient's feelings.

Purification of mind

Tao 도 (道) literally meaning 'the way', the proper way of being itself, signifies the primeval and fundamental principle that underlies everything from the creation of the universe to the interaction of human beings. In Confucianism and religious forms of Taoism, *Tao* is often about proper behaviour and explicitly ethical debates and refers to the cultivation of the mind liberating oneself from any desire or striving; whereas in Buddhism and more philosophical forms of Taoism, it usually refers to the natural and floating way of being, having no attachment and reaching emptiness. In the view of Rhee Dong-Shick, pacifying the mind by eliminating complexes and projection, rectifying cognitive distortion and accepting reality as it is, or anything that seeks the purification of mind and the realisation of truth is, in actuality, *Tao*. This *Tao* is more commonly expressed in its central principle of Wu-wei. Wu-wei 무위 (無爲) literally means 'non-doing', 'non-action', 'non-interference' or 'emptiness'. Far from doing nothing or being passive, Wu-wei is a form of action of 'not acting in conflict with the *Tao*', that is the complete loss of any neurotic desires, striving and attachment, called nuclear feelings in Taopsychotherapy, whereby one reaches the purification of the mind. In Taopsychotherapy, this way of being in the state of Wu-wei is understood as one of the most desirable therapeutic attitudes for a psychotherapist in working with a patient. According to Rhee Dong-Shick, it is crucial for therapists to gain access to the patient's internal psychic life by grasping the subjective meanings that the patient holds of things or experiences. He stresses that by remaining in the state of Wu-wei without disrupting or rupturing the patient's subjectivity, the therapist can effectively attain the patient's subjective meanings and profound minds. The purification of the minds realised through elimination of nuclear feelings and Wu-wei is clearly the essential precondition for the therapists in Taopsychotherapy.

Implication of Taopsychotherapy

Rhee Dong-Shick highlights the fundamental philosophical background in Taopsychotherapy as being aware of reality and accepting reality as it is. Thus, the ultimate goal of Taopsychotherapeutic practice is the removal of projection which creates illusion, and therefore conflict. Rhee Dong-Shick views words, concepts, theories and logic as only the means to reach reality like 'the pointing fingers', and they do not lead to reality. To obtain quickly a patient's subjective and experiential reality, in Taopsychotherapy the therapist first needs to liberate the oneself from the learnt theories and techniques and not to respond to feelings intellectually. According to him, Western psychotherapists who are experienced, competent and free from the so far rigid and inelastic concepts and methodology, would easily comprehend the essence of Taopsychotherapy and within that understanding the integration of Taopsychotherapy and Western psychotherapy is mutually beneficial as they share the same therapeutic goal. In Taopsychotherapy, the successful outcomes of therapy can be attained through the *Tao*. In particular, the practice of *Tao* by the therapist with strong motivation is considered the most important curative factor. Rhee Dong-Shick stresses that while it is difficult to reach the *Tao*, one become more mature as a therapist through the incessant attempts to reach the *Tao*.

Korean Academy of Psychotherapists 1974

In 1974, Rhee Dong-Shick 이동식 (1920–2014) began a weekly Psychotherapy Case Study Group, which developed into the 'Korean psychotherapy research group' in 1976, then the 'Korean Academy of Psychotherapists (KAP)' after 1979. The philosophical goal of the Academy has been to assimilate Western psychoanalysis and psychotherapy to the *Tao* and its Korean cultural roots, and to integrate and unify them. Since 1976 when the KAP became a society member of the International Federation for Psychotherapy (IFP), the members of KAP have actively participated in the world congresses. In 1976, Rhee Dong-Shick presented a paper titled 'Integration of Eastern *Tao* and Western Psychotherapy' at the tenth meeting of the International Federation for Medical Psychotherapy (IFMP, the former International Federation for Psychotherapy – IFP) held in Paris. Since then, KAP members have also conducted several international workshops on 'Integration of Eastern *Tao* and Western Psychotherapy', including those in Bruno, Czechoslovakia and in Moscow, Russia in 1991. The KAP hosted a joint conference with the 'American Academy of Psychoanalysis' in 1990 and with the 'Australia and New Zealand Associations of Psychotherapy' in 1992. In 1994, KAP hosted the sixteenth International Congress of Psychotherapy of IFP in Seoul with the central theme of 'Psychotherapy: East and West'.

The first official use of the name 'Taopsychotherapy' was when the KAP initiated a lecture series titled 'Introduction to Taopsychotherapy' on 1 April 2001. During the World Congress of Psychiatry held in Yokohama, Japan in August 2002, the KAP held a workshop on Taopsychotherapy and this is recognised as the declaration of Taopsychotherapy to the world. Today, a number of young psychiatrists, psychotherapists and trainees are involved in the Academy. Many of them maintain an active practice of some form of Eastern meditation and integrate this into their personal and professional lives. Buddhist and Heideggerian scholars also consistently participate in the activities of the Academy. The KAP regularly holds study groups, case presentations and academic symposiums.

Ten Ox-herding pictures 십우도

The ten Ox-herding pictures (十牛圖), in the tradition of *Seon* Buddhism, are intended to illustrate the stages of a Buddhist practitioner's progression towards enlightenment, as well as one's subsequent perfection of wisdom. Each picture is accompanied by a commentary in prose and verse. The ten Ox-herding pictures have concretely depicted the process by which the absurd, bounded and imperfect ego awakens to the wise, unlimited, and perfect self, and completely integrates into the new nature. In Buddhism, the Ox represents the Buddhahood.

Looking for the Ox, seeing the traces and the Ox (Figures 8.2–1, 2, 3) correspond to understanding the central dynamics i.e., nuclear feelings. At first, these are negative emotions. Catching the Ox (Figure 8.2–4) means being aware of these emotions without repressing them. Herding the Ox (Figure 8.2–5) means being in control of the emotions and resolving the conflicts, with the emerging and growing positive feelings. Coming home on the Ox's back (Figure 8.2–6) is accepting the problem and the reality and resolving the conflicts. Ox lost and man remaining (Figure 8.2–7) means that while conflicts are resolved, the self is not completely transcended. Ox and Man both lost (Figure 8.2–8) is complete non-attachment or emptiness (*sunyata*). This is complete liberation and self-transcendence. Returning to the source (Figure 8.2–9) is seeing oneself and reality as it is without projection or returning to one's original nature. In town with helping hands (Figure 8.2–10) is to become an individual who, having achieved a sense of enlightenment, purity of mind, helps others. The initial series ended with the eighth picture. The series was expanded to its present ten in an effort to elucidate the meaning, that the emptiness of the eighth picture is not nothingness but rather the potential for eternal change.

In the literature on Taopsychotherapy, there are references to these ten Ox-herding pictures. Each of these metaphors is used to evoke experience and awareness on the part of patients, which leads them to a freedom from psychological suffering and constriction. The ten Ox-herding pictures show the process of purification of mind. The symbolic meaning of the Ox is a subject much questioned among Eastern scholars and practitioners. For Rhee Dong-Shick, the Ox represents what he calls the patient's nuclear feeling.[1]

Figure 8.2–1

1. SEEKING THE OX 심우 (尋牛)

In this first picture, the Ox-herder is in a natural setting, his body and feet oriented to the left while his head is turned around facing the right: reminiscent of the ambi-tendency. The Ox-herder knows that there is something missing in his life and more to life. However, he has not yet found the course he wants to pursue. It is the stage when one begins to see one's mind. The desire to seek the essential, original self has arisen.

Figure 8.2–2

2. SEEING THE TRACKS 견적 (見跡)

In this second picture, the Ox-herder finds footprints, signs of the Ox's existence. Here, one comes to an understanding 'conceptually' that the Ox exists. At this stage, one's search is more focused and better oriented. There is a first encounter with the theory and disciplines, which suggests an initial awareness and understanding of the origins of earthly pain and suffering, the essential self. It is the stage when an intellectual insight into one's problems occurs.

Figure 8.2–3

3. SEEING THE OX 견우 (見牛)

In the third picture, the Ox-herder follows the tracks of the Ox, and he is able to finally see the half-hidden Ox that appears among the trees. This indicates that one catches a momentary glimpse of true nature, focuses on it and enthusiastically pursues it. It is the stage of having the first spiritual experience, reaching the source and getting to see the Buddhahood, namely the nuclear feeling in Taopsychotherapy.

Figure 8.2–4

4. CATCHING THE OX 득우 (得牛)

The Ox-herder, in the fourth picture, exerts himself for catching the wild Ox with a rope. However, the Ox does not want to be caught. As the Ox fights the Ox-herder, he has to hang on tightly as he is being dragged along on the ground. Symbolically, the picture depicts the struggle which occurs as a result of not fully transcending one's passions and desires, between one's true nature and one's desires. It illustrates the gradual awakening of the individual towards their original true self. At this stage, it is important to analyse if one intends to grasp a meaning of spiritual practice or just tries to take shelter in ideas or doctrines. This is the stage when one actively keeps the awareness of nuclear feeling without repressing it.

Figure 8.2–5

5. HERDING THE OX 목우 (牧友)

In this fifth picture, the Ox-herder is lightly taming the Ox. The struggle seems to be over but he still holds the rope in his hand. It depicts that one needs to brace oneself against a wandering mind and to persist in practice. At this stage, one should devote to keep the Ox under control to the utmost and not to have it go off. It teaches to remain united with the essence of self through adhering to strenuous sitting and continual training and dismissing any delusive thoughts and desire like boasting or the experience of wanting to lead others. It is the stage when one works through both negative and positive feelings and develops constructive behavioural patterns.

Figure 8.2–6

6. RIDING THE OX HOME 기우귀가 (騎牛歸家)

In the sixth picture, the Ox-herder is comfortably riding on the back of the Ox as he makes his way back home. There is harmony between the Ox-herder and the Ox. He is no longer restrained or limited by the world. At this stage, one is in control of one's mind and remains awakened. Now with joy and contentment in the heart and mind, one returns 'home' to the true self. This is the stage when one almost removes one's nuclear feelings.

7. OX LOST, MAN REMAINING 망우존인 (忘牛存人)

Figure 8.2–7

In this seventh picture, the Ox-herder at peace is left all alone sitting at home and the Ox disappears. The Ox is forgotten, and the Ox-herder experiences transcendence of the self in the stillness that is an exceptional state of consciousness. Transcendence is a recurring and temporal experience of unity, beyond dualities and self-consciousness still remains as a residue. At this stage, one's nuclear feeling is completely removed and one becomes highly mature. Rhee Dong-Shick views that coming to a place of self-control and a sense of self-fulfilment or self-realisation such as one finds in this seventh picture, is as far as Western psychotherapy can lead the individual patient.

8. MAN AND OX BOTH LOST 인우구망 (人牛俱忘)

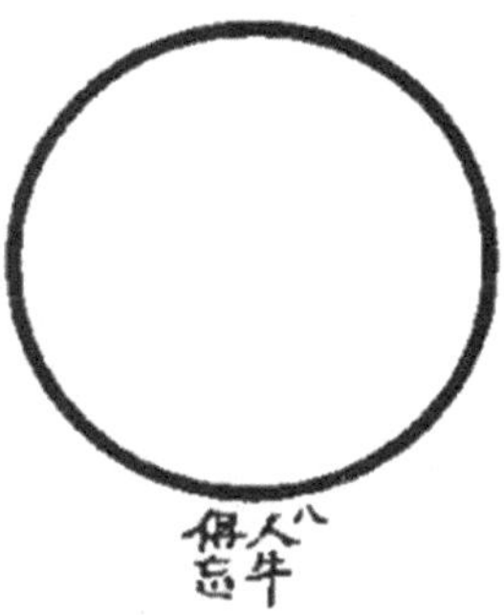

Figure 8.2–8

Now, in the eighth picture, both the Ox and the Ox-herder disappear and are forgotten leaving only an empty circle. The 'emptiness' is attained by forgetting both the Ox and the self. One awakens to the realisation that all arises from emptiness through which one achieves the highest stage of total unity, that of enlightenment. At this stage, one's mind has no attachment.

9. RETURNING TO THE SOURCE 반본환원 (返本還源)

Figure 8.2–9

In this ninth picture, there is no Ox, nor the Ox-herder, and only a pastoral picture that illustrates the scene of the original pure mind. At this stage, one realises that the eighth stage of 'Man and Ox both forgotten' is the essential state of human beings and everything expresses itself as a true reality of life. Now, one sees things as they are without one's own projections and returns to the initial starting point.

Figure 8.2–10

10. IN TOWN WITH HELPING HANDS 입전수수 (入鄽垂手)

In this tenth picture, the Ox-herder, now enlightened man, goes to the village (the mundane world) to help other beings. It is to return to the existential world with a simple, clear and unattached mind that focuses on perceiving the correct relationship and situation in each moment with great compassion. This last picture depicts the core of Buddhist and *Tao* teaching. In Taopsychotherapy, this image of Bodhisattva is considered representing an ideal psychotherapist.

Seon **psychotherapy** 선 심리치료

Seon 선 is a Korean term for the Chinese word 'Chan 禪' that originally derived from the Sanskrit *dhyana* which means 'meditative state' or 'meditation'. 'Chan' that is a form of Mahayana Buddhism was gradually introduced into Korea between the seventh and ninth centuries and to Japan in the twelfth century. In the Occident, Zen 禅 of the Japanese pronunciation is more commonly understood. *Seon* Buddhism has grown in Korea under the distinctive cultural and spiritual integration of Buddhism, Confucianism and Taoism. Its highest aim is self-realisation, a return to real self or true nature, which is comparable to the ultimate objective of psychotherapy.

Seon psychotherapy refers to both the psychotherapy based upon the spiritual understanding of Buddhist philosophy and psychotherapeutic approaches using meditation as an essential component in the process. *Seon* psychotherapy emerges from the desperate need for Korean counselling or psychotherapy that is more appropriate for Korean people. It is stimulated by an upsurge of interest in psychotherapy by Korean *Seon* Buddhist scholars and meditation experts, as well as high interest of mental health professionals in *Seon* teaching and meditation. Rhee Dong-Shick, who had played the leading role in the efforts in attempting to understand the Buddhist thoughts in the perspective of psychotherapy since the 1970s, proclaimed that there is only a subtle difference between psychotherapy and *Seon* Buddhism for the ultimate aim for both is to eliminate illusion and become aware of reality. Since the 1980s, the continuous efforts and studies have persisted in grafting *Seon* spirits onto psychotherapy in Korea.

Dong-Sa-Sub 동사섭 can be considered as its first attempt. *Dong-Sa-Sub* is a name of both the organisation and the group programme initiated by Venerable YongTah 용타 스님 (1942–). The word *Dong-Sa-Sub* (同事攝) refers to one of the Four Virtues practised by Bodhisattva to save the laity. Bodhisattva may perform, depending on circumstance, unselfish service (보시섭; 布施攝), use loving and caring speech (애어섭; 愛語攝), undertake benefit-giving actions (이행섭; 利行攝), or share joy, anger, love and happiness (동사섭; 同事攝). Based upon the understanding that the universe as a unitary, living organism is sustained only by interdependent and mutually complementing actions of its members all playing their rightful roles, *Dong-Sa-Sub* took the last practice of sharing joy, anger, love and happiness as its foundation and the other three as harmoniously supporting concepts. Venerable YongTah who is the founder and chair of *Dong-Sa-Sub* previously attended a programme named T-Group workshop in Gwangju, Korea and discovered the spiritual value in the workshop where participants gained insights into themselves and others through their interaction with each other using feedback, problem solving and role play. It motivated him to set up *Dong-Sa-Sub* adapting modern psychology and counselling methods and theories to *Seon* teaching and practices. *Dong-Sa-Sub* held its first workshop and retreat in 1980. Since then, it has been conducting training workshops and retreats for groups. Started as an unstructured encounter group, it gradually developed into a more structured group for mind training through transcendental meditation. Influenced by *Dong-Sa-Sub*, many programmes in the same spirit have sprung up amongst Buddhist organisations.

In 2000, the term 'Buddhist Counselling 불교상담' first appeared with the establishment of the 'Korean Buddhism Counselling Development Centre (KBCDC) 불교상담 개발원' by the Jogye Order, the representative order of Korean Buddhism. It aimed to research, develop and support Buddhist counselling theories, methods and activities. Lee Keun-Hu 이근후 (1935–), an ardent Buddhist and psychiatrist, presided over the Centre and began the very first Buddhist counselling service. Later, he launched the service that provided phone as well as cyber counselling. Considering his activities as the way to the Buddhist asceticism, Lee Keun-Hu is an eminent figure in the history of Korean psychotherapy with a Buddhist mind. Also as an authority in the field of family and marital relations, he has written and translated around 30 books which include various clinical cases accessible to general readers. Since 2008, the KBCDC has been producing Buddhist counselling therapists, and 151 people had been trained by 2010.

In 2002, Inkyung Sunim 인경스님, who was trained in Religious psychology and Transpersonal transcendental psychology in the United States, opened the 'Institute of *Seon* Counselling'. The universities of Dongguk, Dongbang, Joong-ang Sangha and Seoul Buddhism also started courses on Buddhism counselling or meditation therapy from 2003. In 2007, the 'Korean Association of Buddhism and Psychotherapy (KABP) 한국 불교 심리치료 협회' was established by six professionals in Buddhism, psychiatry and psychology including Master Misan Sunim, Kim Jae-Sung, Yun Ho-Kyun, Jeong Hyun-Su, Seo Dong Hyeok and Jo Sung-Ho, and the term 'Buddhist Psychotherapy 불교 심리치료' came into use.

Meditation psychotherapy 명상심리치료

Among the monks who attempt to integrate the doctrine of Buddhism into psychotherapy is Inkyung Sunim 인경스님 (1956–). Since 2002, he has endeavoured to interpret literary documents of Buddhism in the light of psychotherapy and develop programmes for counselling or psychotherapy focused on Buddhist

Figure 8.3 Inkyung Sunim

meditation for the general public. Since 2005, he has begun to apply the programmes. In 2007, he established the 'Korean Meditation Therapy Association 한국 명상치료 학회' whose name was changed to the 'Korean Meditation Counselling Association 한국 명상상담 학회' in 2013, and has been more actively involved in researching and training of meditation counselling experts.

The representative concepts of Buddhism that Inkyung Sunim introduces to meditation psychotherapy are *Yogacara* 유식 (唯識), *Hwadu* 화두 (話頭) and *Go-Jip-Myeol-Do* 고집멸도 (苦集滅道). The programmes have been well received with a gradual increase of interest and participation of the general public. In 2012, he published a book entitled *Meditation Psychotherapy: An Integrative Study on Buddhist Meditation and Psychotherapy*. This is the first book written on meditation psychotherapy in Korea introducing methods and cases in which these methods were successfully applied.

Yogacara *meditation*

Yogacara Buddhism is known to have the most abundant psychological contents which involve detailed descriptions of psychic structures and functions. Commonly known as 'Consciousness-only (*yogacara*)', the fundamental doctrine of the *Yogacara* School is that all phenomenal existence is fabricated by consciousness. *Yogacara* Buddhism explains the human psychic phenomena by the seed theory and the transformation of consciousnesses. It is that Mind comes into 'contact 접촉 (觸)' with an object, which activates a 'seed 작의 (作意)' or motif, sequentially producing 'feeling 감정 (受)', 'thought 생각 (想)' and 'desire 갈망 (行)'.

These feelings, thoughts and desires generate suffering. To liberate the mind from suffering, the mind needs to transcend these general mental phenomena. According to Inkyung Sunim, to enable to create the transformation of mind, the repressed or ignored 'feeling' should be thoroughly explored, confronted and purified; the obsessed or fixed 'thought' be examined; the frustrated and rejected 'desire' be expressed and altered by another effective behaviour.

By integrating the understanding of Mind of *Yogacara* Buddhism with some approaches to psychotherapy, Inkyung Sunim systematised a programme of meditation psychotherapy called 'Changing the Mind 마음 바꾸기'. It is composed of the next four steps. First, it starts with 'Breathing' and '*Yeom-Ji-Gwan* Meditation' that manages feelings. The second step is 'LIDA Meditation' focused on changing thoughts. The third step is '*Yeom-Ji-Gwan* Meditation' related to changing feeling through reflected image. The final step is 'Self-Transcendence *Hwadu* Meditation'. *Yogacara* 유식 (唯識) Meditation Psychotherapy refers to the first three methods.

Yeom-Ji-Gwan *meditation*

Yeom-Ji-Gwan 염지관 (念止觀) is the state of first becoming aware of a bodily feeling and the phenomenon of mind conditioned by that feeling, then wholly experiencing it by calmly accepting it and lastly contemplating it. '*Yeom* 염 (念)' refers

Figure 8.4 *Yeom-Ji-Gwan* meditation therapy (Awareness–Stay–Observation Meditation); workshop held in Beobryun-sa © July 2012 The Korean Meditation Counselling Association

to the Pali term *sati* meaning 'awareness'. According to the Buddhist teaching, this is a spiritual capacity that is considered to be of prime importance in the path toward enlightenment. As the Chinese character 念 which is composed of 今 meaning 'now' or 'this' and 心 meaning 'heart' or 'mind' suggests, *Yeom* is to have an awareness and acceptance of mental phenomena as felt in the present moment. The concepts of *Ji* and *Gwan* are regarded as the essence of Buddhist meditation. '*Ji* 지 (止)' refers to *samatha* in Sanskrit, which means 'stop to end', 'cease to rise' or 'calm to rest'. It is an act of concentration on a particular object or idea, aimed at calming the mind by putting an end to erroneous thinking. '*Gwan* 관 (觀)' that is *vipassana* means 'contemplate', insight into the true nature of reality, the inseparability of appearance and emptiness, the impermanence of everything that exists.

In *Yeom-Ji-Gwan* Meditation, *Yeom*, '알아차림 *al-a-cha-lim*' in the Korean term, is to bring awareness to the feelings transmitted through the six senses. At the stage of *Ji*, '머물기 *meo-mul-gi*', to confront the object and the entailed feeling without avoiding or repressing it is considered to be most important. It is to stop any action or pause in experiencing the feeling itself, concentrating on the object and calmly abiding. *Gwan*, '지켜보기 *ji-kyeo-bo-gi*', is to observe movement in the object or any change and dissolution of the feeling. First, it is to observe 'my' reactions to pleasant or unpleasant feelings, the increasing desire or craving for pleasurable sensations or the fear or avoidance of the uncomfortable sensations. In this process, one becomes aware of 'suffering 고 (苦)', i.e., *dukkha*. Second, it is to observe the changes in feeling without having to go along with the reactions of desire or avoidance, and to experience that none of the feelings is sustained for long but dissolves. This experience is indispensable for insight into the 'impermanent 무상 (無常)', i.e., *anicca*, in that all of conditioned existence is in a constant state of flux. Inkyung Sunim cautions that one moves to another object only after having observed the change and dissolution of the captured feeling about the object. Third, it is to observe that 'I' or 'mine' as an object does not exist. All things perceived by the senses including the mental sense of myself are not really 'I' or 'mine', and for this reason one should not cling to them. This is to realise the illusion of self or 'non-self 무아 (無我)', i.e., *anatta*.

Yeom-Ji-Gwan Meditation Therapy is especially focused on the observation of feelings. The occurrence of feeling is the objective of *Yeom*, the pause of feeling is *Ji* and the change and dissolution of feeling corresponds to *Gwan*. Since 2007, case studies on various groups of elderly, married women, young children, adolescents or soldiers have been conducted contributing to the development of *Yeom-Ji-Gwan* Meditation Therapy. It is officially translated into 'Awareness–Stay–Observation Meditation (ASOM)' in English.

LIDA *meditation*

Inkyung Sunim develops *LIDA* Meditation Therapy 리다 명상치료 by integrating some techniques of cognitive behavioural therapy and acceptance–commitment therapy. It is to name the feeling arising in mind and to bring the change in thought. First, one notices and becomes aware of a certain feeling and puts a 'label (L)' to the feeling. As a second step, one makes 'inquiry (I)' into the feeling and the thoughts. At the third stage, one 'defuses (D)' the feeling. Finally, it involves 'accepting and acting (A)' according to the newly realised value or belief.

Youngsang-Gwan *meditation*

Youngsang-Gwan 영상관 (影像觀) Meditation translated into 'Reflected Image Meditation (RIM)' sets itself the task of trying to attain elaborate insight on the unsolved issues by reflecting on the concerned image or scene. An incident of the past does not disappear but is stored in the mind as a schema or seed in the form of an image. *Youngsang-Gwan* Meditation Therapy is to evoke this image by deliberately making it rise to the surface of the mind. Then it involves calmly observing the image without any attempt to take control or get rid of it, until one realises that the image is only driven by one's consciousness and inexistent in reality, thus eventually transcendable. This reflected image refers to *pratibimba* in Sanskrit.

Youngsang-Gwan 영상관 Meditation Therapy follows the next procedure: The first stage is to comprehend the task such as an unsolved problem, related incident or a concrete scene related to personal experience for exploration. The second stage involves re-experiencing the situation by recalling any chosen scenes or images. The counsellor can guide the patient to thoroughly examine the image arising from the senses for a vivid re-experience by asking questions like 'What do you hear or see?', 'What do you look like?', 'Who is with you?', and so on. The third stage is to retrieve what is re-experienced by clarifying particularly the feeling, the thought and the desire of the contents. The fourth stage is to intervene in the reflected image of the situation, express what was repressed or try to invoke an alternative behaviour: 'What would you like to do if you could go back to that situation?' This stage provides an opportunity to resolve the problem by executing a new creative form of behaviour by intervention. The fifth and final stage is to obtain insight into the essence of objects. It is to return to the initial reflected image, only watch it objectively and notice any changes in feelings. Inkyung Sunim further suggests that the use of psychodrama around the elicited images can be beneficial.

Hwadu *meditation*

In the practice of '*Hwadu* 화두 (話頭) Meditation (HM)', one is given a 'topic of inquiry', i.e., *Hwadu* and led to focus all of one's attention on examining the *Hwadu*. In therapy, *Hwadu* can be an emerging feeling. As the inquiry into one's *Hwadu* deepens through intensive meditation and dialogue, the mind's inability to understand the meaning of the *Hwadu* creates an intense questioning, what the *Seon* tradition calls the 'sense of doubt'. The doubt is so intensified that one's mind is absorbed in the *Hwadu*, questioning flows continuously and effortlessly, and one enters a single-minded state where one is oblivious to everything in one's life except this questioning. It is at this breaking point that 'the self', which limits one's point-of-view, is transcended and the mind opens to the boundless perspective of enlightenment. *Hwadu* Meditation was previously called Self-Transcendence *Ganhwa-Seon* 간화선 (看話禪) Meditation Therapy.

Go-Jip-Myeol-Do *meditation*

Inkyung Sunim developed the '*Go-Jip-Myeol-Do* 고집멸도 (苦集滅道) Meditation Therapy' programme in which the focus lays more in Buddhist counselling. *Go-Jip-Myeol-Do* is one of the central teachings of Buddhism of the four noble truths that explain the nature of suffering, its causes and how it can be overcome. If one understands the truth that all is suffering, that suffering originates in accumulation, that all suffering disappears and that there is the Way to eliminate suffering, then one can be called a gracious and holy person. Inkyung Sunim interprets this teaching in terms of psychotherapy and presents it as one method of mediation psychotherapy integrating the Enneagram of personality and J. Young's Schema Questionnaire.

In *Go-Jip-Myeol-Do* Meditation Therapy, the first stage of empathy and support is to share and understand 'suffering (*Go* 고; 苦). The second stage of clarification is to define and identify its origins and causes, that is the 'accumulation (*Jip* 집; 集)'. The third stage of insight is to 'dissipate (*Myeol* 멸; 滅)', the stage at which symptoms of suffering fades away and there is spiritual experience. The fourth stage of practising the Way is on the 'noble path (*Do* 도; 道)' that frees one from suffering. This stage is defined as a process of exploring new behaviour and putting it into practice in day-to-day life.

Onmaum counselling 온마음 상담

Yun Ho-Kyun 윤호균 (1942–) trained as a psychologist in the 1960s and has endeavoured to integrate Eastern philosophical thoughts into the practice of counselling since the beginning of the 1970s. While still a student majoring in psychology, he developed his general interest in Eastern philosophies and religions, and took part in the study group led by Rhee Dong-Shick, the founder of Taopsychotherapy. Gradually, he came to the realisation that there was a great potential to integrate Eastern philosophy into counselling. He produced several articles on 'Buddhism and Counselling' with a particular interest in the notion of Buddha Nature (佛性; True Self) and the Buddhist concept of *pratityasamutpaada* 연기론 (緣起論; dependent origination). He introduced the '*Onmaum* (Whole-Mind) Counselling 온마음 상담' as a counselling model from the viewpoint of Buddhism.

The three essential mechanisms of *Onmaum* counselling are: one's full acceptance of oneself and experiences, one's clear awareness of imagination and one's free disidentification from experiences. According to Buddhism, the reality of an individual is a construction of one's own experience that derives from imagination which reflects one's history, concepts, knowledge and expectations. Accordingly, the reality of an individual is inevitably attributed to the construction of one's own experience. In *Onmaum* counselling, therefore, becoming aware of one's illusory reality and to be free from it is essential, and an *Onmaum* counsellor needs to establish a counselling environment in which the patient's subjective reality can be freely and genuinely expressed.

Hence, Yun Ho-Kyun stresses the counsellors' wholehearted listening, accepting, empathising and awakening the patient's experiences and True Self. Resting upon the counsellor's full understanding and acceptance of their experiences and feelings, patients can explore and understand what facts and imaginations (or projections) contribute to the construction of their own reality. The counsellor helps them to understand their desires and fears to which most of the problem-generating imagination is related, and to realise the fact that they have created their imagined reality and problems mostly by their own projections, attachments or identifications. This awareness and full realisation of their illusory reality generated by their imaginations helps them to be free from the identifications with their own perceptions, feelings, thoughts, desires, etc. It allows patients to obtain disidentification that is comparable to the concept of *anatta* (무아, 無我; Non-Self) of Buddhism, and thus their True Self. Yun Ho-Kyun proclaims that *Onmaum* counselling should be a method not only appropriate for Koreans but for all, and he is reluctant to refer to it solely as Korean psychotherapy. Stressing on the importance of each counsellor's constant personal work on the self, he warns of the fallacy to postpone one's own awareness and experience to Western theoretical concepts in practices.

Among the psychologists whose works are orientated in this direction, that is in the use of Buddhist meditation as an effective means to promote an increase in health and beneficial changes in life, there are noticeably Jang Hyun-Gab 장현갑 (1942–), the first to attempt to integrate psychology, neuroscience and meditation through introducing 'Integrative Medicine'; Kwon Seok-Man 권석만 (1958–) particularly suggesting '*Samhak* 삼학 (三學: Three Studies)' that is Discipline, Mediation and Wisdom for self-healing; and Kim Jung-Ho 김정호 (1958–) who uses Mindfulness Meditation in addition to positive psychology in his practice. As a psychiatrist who is actively involved in applying Buddhist meditation in clinical practices, Jeon Hyun-Su 전현수 (1956–) is representative. Presenting it as '*Maum* Therapy', he regularly runs eight-week programmes of 'meditation and self-healing' for the general public.

Notes

1 Erik Craig, an American psychologist presented a paper in 2005 in which he talked of a remarkably close analogue in these first seven pictures to Heidegger's thought found in

Being and Time: Beginning with the questioning of Being (Figure 8.2–1, 2), the discovery of human existence, i.e. Dasein (Figure 8.2–3), the struggle with the fundamental conditions of human existence (Figure 8.2–4, 5, 6), and the realisation of *Gelassenheit*, generally translated as equanimity or serenity, or the capacity to what is to 'be' (Figure 8.2–7).

2 The general or universal definition of *pratiityasamutpaada* is that everything arises in dependence upon multiple causes and conditions; nothing exists as a singular, independent entity. The Twelve *Nidaanas* ('cause, foundation, source or origin') are an application of *pratiityasamutpaada*. They identify the origin of *dukkha* (suffering) to be in *avijja* (ignorance). The Twelve-fold chains are: Ignorance 무명(無明) – Formation 행(行) – Consciousness 식(識) – Name and Form 명색(名色) – Six Sense Gate 육입(六入) – Contact 촉(觸) – Feeling (Sensation) 수(受) – Craving 애(愛) – Attachment 취(取) – Becoming 유(有) – Birth 생(生) – Ageing, Deca, and Death 노사(老死).

3 The first concerns the study of Discipline (계; 戒) on body and mind, which is word, deed or thought. The second is the study on Mediation (정; 定), that is the cultivation of compassion. The third is the study of Wisdom (혜; 慧), that is learning of principle and solving of doubts.

Bibliography

Erik, C. (2005, August). *Taopsychotherapy: Integrating psychoanalytic, humanistic, existential and transpersonal perspectives.* Paper presented at the 113th Annual Convention of the American Psychological Association, Washington.

Huh, C. H. (2003, September). *Taopsychotherapy.* Paper presented at the 14th International symposium for the psychological treatment of schizophrenia and other psychoses, Melbourne.

Inkyung (2007). Buddhist spirituality and meditation-therapy. *Meditation Therapy Studies*, 1, 135–163. [Korean]

Inkyung (2008). Implication of IBMM, *Meditation Therapy Studies*, 2: 61–89. [Korean]

Inkyung (2010). The four noble truths in counselling and psychotherapeutic understanding. *Korean Sean Studies*, 2, 1–26. [Korean]

Inkyung (2012). *Meditation Psychotherapy: an integrative study on Buddhist meditation and psychotherapy*. Seoul: Institute of Meditation Counselling. [Korean]

Kang, S. H. (1990). Training and development of psychotherapy in Korea. *Psychotherapy and Psychosomatics*, 53, 46–49.

Kim, H. R. (2007). Buddhism Meditation: A comparative study on Vipassana and Ganwha Meditation. *Dongbang Journal*, 1, 239–256.

Kim, M. W. (2008). A comparative study of MBSR (Mindfulness Based Stress Reduction) and Sati-Samatha & Vipassana. *Meditation Therapy Studies*, 2, 7–60. [Korean]

Oh, Y. K. (2007). A study on group counselling by Breath meditation and Yeom-Ji-Gwan meditation. *Meditation Therapy Studies*, 1, 249–300. [Korean]

Park, J. S. (2003). A Study on Seon therapy methods. *Journal of Korean Sean Studies*, 6, 219–248. [Korean]

Rhee, D. S. (1970). Research on Psychotherapy of Korean Patients. *New Medical Journal*, 1 (9), 77–101. [Korean]

Rhee, D. S. (1976). *Process of the Tao practice and psychotherapy*. Paper presented to the 10th Meeting of the International Federation for Medical Psychotherapy, Paris, France.

Rhee, D. S. (1979). *The Tao and Western Psychotherapy.* Paper presented to the 11th Meeting of the International Federation for Medical Psychotherapy, Amsterdam, Netherlands.

Rhee, D. S. (2008). *Introduction to Taopsychotherapy: Beyond Freud and Jung.* Seoul: Hangangsu. [Korean]
Yun, H. K. (2001). Imagination, Clinging, and Counselling. *Korean Journal of Counselling and Psychotherapy*, 13 (3), 1–18. [Korean]
Yun, H. K. (2005). The Mechanism of Onmaum Counselling. *Korean Journal of Counselling and Psychotherapy*, 17 (13), 1–13. [Korean]
Yun, H. K. (2007). Onmaum Counselling. *Korean Journal of Counselling and Psychotherapy,* 19(3), 505–522. [Korean]

Conclusion

Saturated with ephemeral and ready-made knowledge on how to treat the mind, Korean psychotherapy has effected a breakout today discovering a lead in the therapeutic precedents set in Korean history. It has gradually recovered its autochthonous character providing the same effectiveness today as it did in the old times. Archaeological knowledge has shown that Koreans had had their autonomous ways for curing the mind illnesses, without a concept and care for mental health as defined by Western knowledge.

Knowledge in pledge

Individuals, communities and society are all a historical product of the cultural, ethical and spiritual milieus, constructed by those in power. Knowledge itself cannot be understood outside of its historical and social context and knowledge about one's history cannot be obtained outside of its socio-political structural frame within each period. Thus, a knowledge applied without consideration of the autochthonous will lack legitimacy. Having passed through the colonial regime of Japan and the hegemony of the United States, Koreans simply absorbed knowledge transmitted by the Japanese and the Americans, instead of going through prudent assimilation of the new knowledge. Koreans have been exposed to this knowledge ever since 1910 when the Japanese government took control of Korea. The autochthonous were mostly despised or neglected, while professionals were busy adapting the knowledge obtained in such manner to Korean practice. The history of modern knowledge and practice of psychotherapy in Korea draws upon the same intellectual line and the adequate development of psychotherapy appropriate for people and culture of Korea has been hindered.

Integration amiss

Indeed, Korea experienced political, social and cultural discontinuity owing to the influence of Japanese colonialism, the Korean War, the divided Korea, rapid modernisation and the indiscriminate influx of American culture. Under Japanese colonialism, the culprit in the harm of the mind was the strict restraint and severe oppression placed upon Korean people in every activity of their daily life. During the postwar period, the split of political ideology, territorial division and ethnic confrontation were largely responsible for widespread existential and mental instability. The American 'civilisation' that followed seriously reinforced the dichotomy between the material and the immaterial. Under these circumstances, there could no longer exist traditional independent beings living in harmony within collective society, but just dependent beings living with an obsession about 'norms ruled under the panoptic surveillance'[1] and control over the very Korean mind by inlanders as much as by outlanders.

Koreans who had undergone the complete loss of sovereignty and the subsequent impoverishment created by the war, have flocked to American ideals and institutions after the war – desperately running after material wealth and success as a compensation for the deprived past. Since the 1950s, they have tried desperately and uniformly to make a breakthrough for their existence through modernisation and westernisation. The military and dictatorial regime of Park Jung-Hi (1917–1979) in effect between 1963 and 1979 enforced it further by focusing only on economic revival and disregarding ethical and spiritual values. The speedy transformation of living conditions to a modernised and industrialised life was definitely a fruitful compensation. Nonetheless, it was only a displacement from the ruthless Japanese government to a crafty American guidance; from one cast of colonialism that ceased any creation to another cast of materialism that mass-produced automata. Without a veritable independence, modernised Koreans have 'willingly' pursued the norm, in order words, 'the identical' – do likewise in every way of life. What was imposed and justified was then accepted as natural, inevitable, perpetual and beneficial for everyone. Such modern Koreans have been mostly preoccupied with accumulation and possession under a delusion about raison d'être and happiness.

Floundering in a quagmire

Today, Koreans are still living in a blend of these circumstances of no less than colonialism, war and dictatorship: they suffer under the 'imperialist' system ruled by Capital and the elite, from the fierce war of rivalry for success and the absolute power of mammon. Excessive academic elitism, careerism, extravagance and ostentation owing to the increased emphasis on social status and appearance, servile imitation of Western culture and erosion of traditional support networks such as relatives, friends or villagers are not only leading to dehumanisation and community sprit breakdown, but also deepening the social and emotional disparity between the haves and the have-nots. Anger and frustration at unequal socio-economic conditions, relative poverty, sense of alienation and despair are pervasive. Since the financial crisis of 1997, which caused the massive growth of the homeless, the unemployed and the poor, the sudden increase in the broken family and the spread of anxiety and despair, social polarisation is increasingly aggravated in contemporary Korea. Now it is seriously affecting the mental health of Korean people.[2] Modern Korea quickly built, thus structurally unsound, starts groaning under the weight. Violence, greed, split and isolation are only a few examples of malaise afflicting contemporary Korea. Mental poverty is an inevitable side-effect of materialism and drives many Koreans to abandon their beliefs, ethics and humanity and even take their own life or that of others', making Korea today a country with the highest suicide rate[3] and also coining the new phrase of 'do not ask (why) murder' that is, impulsive killing of innocent people with no preconceived motivation.

Unwilling seeker: individuals

Nevertheless, Koreans are reluctant or unwilling to seek help from mental health professionals.[4] The experts unanimously agree on the three reasons for this. Above all, Koreans have a largely negative opinion about mental health care because of the social stigma attached to mental treatment. Anyone who may seek psychiatric or psychological help is easily condemned as a problem, a nuisance, a personal failure or a severe deficiency. Next, there is a stereotypical view that seeking help is shameful. It is an assumed sign of weakness particularly when it concerns a mental illness that is still very much a taboo in daily conversation. Lastly, getting proper psychotherapy from professionals is costly, as it is not covered by insurance. It demotivates people from getting psychotherapeutic help.

Moreover, Koreans are reluctant to talk about their personal problems to a stranger. Thus, speaking of their issues to a therapist who is a complete stranger is very uncomfortable for them. When going through turbulent times, Koreans had turned mostly to their family, friends, teachers or spiritual leaders for advice or guidance in dealing with their personal difficulties including the mental issues. This way of seeking help remains predominant. Even in some serious cases, they often consult a physician only for medical support and prefer to avoid leaving any trace of possible mental treatment in their medical history. In addition, they tend to disregard any effect of verbal therapy with the fixed idea that an illness of the mind cannot be cured by 'just talking with another person'. Such inability or unwillingness to recognise their root issues obviously worsens the symptoms and prevents them from getting proper help.

Intervention beyond reach: government

Before the 1970s, within rural communities of an extended family system, the mentally-ill lived their life well next to the family and were relatively integrated into their local communities. It had not yet come to the fore as a social burden or problem. From the 1970s, Korea radically transformed from an agricultural to a capitalist industrial society and the rapid industrialisation and urbanisation accelerated the rise of the nuclear family. Under this change, the mentally-ill became more or less a nuisance to family and society. Isolated and neglected without adequate treatment and basic livelihood security, some got involved in violence and crimes. Reports by media exaggerated the cases and the social prejudices against the mentally-ill so that 'the mad are dangerous' dictum became intensified.

The poor mental health system, the lack of psychiatric wards, and the inadequacy of medical social security left them in the hands of unauthorised personnel to supervise them. The Christian communities that had acquired a dramatic expansion by then fulfilled this social need for quarantine of the mentally-ill. They opened many unauthorised prayer houses and started accommodating them. Entering the 1980s, the notoriety for their inhumane surveillance and mistreatment appalled the public which induced governmental intervention to expand psychiatric hospitals and the care system. However, the abuse by these religious groups was an unresolved issue and the public care systems were still caught short. The Mental Health Act of 1997 tended to a general improvement in the services and the public awareness of the human rights of the mentally-ill. And yet, the government subsidies and intervention did not meet the demands of the mentally ill people and their families in need of support. In many cases, the immediate family was still the prime, if not only, support for those who suffer from the mental illnesses. For those without 'severe' mental health issues not requiring hospitalisation, care and treatment were incredibly limited. Besides, the socio-structural problems deepened by unequal distribution of wealth and power went on to provoke an increasing mental impoverishment and degeneration.

Misguided training institutions: professionals

Korean mass media finally reacted. It started producing reports on mental health issues. Mental health experts also appeared on television and in magazines, thus catching the public's attention. Psychiatric hospitals held lectures that were open to the public. The media certainly contributed to popularising the term 'depression (우울; *Uoul*)'. Simultaneously, it inspired a number of young graduates to pursue further education and a career as a mental health professional that was not necessarily medical. Quickly, it led to a boom in the 2000s and many training institutions were established to comply with this request. As mentioned above, most of these training institutions provide relevant certificates issued by each related association. They are private qualifications. Each different association of Western psychotherapeutic orientations states its evaluation criteria for qualification. There are usually three levels classed largely depending on the number of years of practice. To upgrade a level of qualification, applicants need to complete certain courses, usually offered by the same organisation that issues the certificate. In addition, they have to pay each time for an exam, certificate, registration and membership. The grander associations have local branches around the country. Even those who complete academic training at master's level at university usually seek to obtain such a certificate for an additional validation.

At the core of Foucault's picture of modern 'disciplinary' society are three primary methods of societal control: hierarchical observation, normalising judgement and the examination. The associations and certificates prevailing in Korea regrettably draw on this model of modern disciplinary system. They become a vehicle of effective control over the mass-production of 'standardised' therapists whose roles are subordinate to the disciplines offered by each association. In reality, the demand for therapy is far from sufficient to meet the supply of these therapists and the public do not seem to respond well to Western knowledge and skills acquired within the artificial institutional constructs.

Ssial: counter-cultural hegemony

Turning to the twenty-first century, there seems to be a gradual awakening to a life of automaton operated by the identical codes borrowed from other cultures. The newly awakened Koreans attempt to save the 'difference' shadowed by the norm that fundamentally pursues 'the identical'.[5] In a way, it is a revelation of the invisible deprivation of the intrinsic culture over the past 100 years, a resumption of the indigenous lifestyle, the cultural practices and the traditional thoughts and beliefs at the present history. In Korea, perhaps like any other country, artists have been the only constant group that has sustained, and allowed the historical and traditional to flourish, while at the same time questioning and resisting the ruling 'norms'. These artists belong to '*Ssial*' as the oppressed, marginalised ordinary group of people who are, nevertheless, at the source of creative life. For Nietzsche, artists are the inventors of new possibilities of life, who create new ways of being and perceiving. Today, increasingly artists integrate traditional Korean moves, rhythms, sounds and stories into their work, creating new potentials for Korea that has lost its singularity in the lifestyles brought in from the outside. It appeals to more and more people. Koreans newly identify with their traditional heritage and resist the implicit consensus to the cultural values of the West. It is on one hand, a resistance to the cultural hegemony and on the other hand, a reconciling gesture for reunion with and a path to recovery of the intrinsic.

Antonio Gramsci's 'cultural hegemony' is the concept that a society of varied cultures can be easily controlled by one social group over another, that shared beliefs and daily practices furnish the cornerstone for a structure of control. He claims that the ruled need to develop a counter-hegemonic culture, first by overthrowing the notion that the ruling values represented natural or normal values for society, then by offering fundamental and long-term resistance. Nietzsche pointed out that it is by virtue of artistic creativity that Man can justify his existence, and give meaning and direction to it. Deleuze stated that through art, one can see the circumstances, understand the essential differences and recognise the real as the world of change and becoming. According to him, expression is opposed to representation which remains in a form of the identical. Expression is to embrace change, make difference and form the creation, and it is the power that makes the invisible visible. In this regard, expressive arts therapy is to create something different by way of an original unique style of interpretation of experiences embodied through artistic expression. In psychotherapy as in any other areas, what was considered effective for Westerners was adopted, adapted and taken as read by Korean therapists. Such knowledge imposed on practice without interrogation since the introduction is now being reviewed at the autochthonous position. Today, Korean psychotherapy finds a cue in the autochthonous practices of arts play and expressive art therapy integrating traditional artistic activities, and conduces to making a step towards a counter-hegemonic culture in the milieu of Korean psychotherapy.

Indigenous knowledge

In this book, the spirit of *Pungryu* was highlighted as the essence of natural lifestyle and a fundamental framework for the Korean philosophy of life. It reflects not only the autochthonous practices of arts play that generates the joy and the oneness but also the social consciousness for justice and freedom. On the basis of the notion that *Pungryu* is profoundly embedded in the Korean psyche as the innermost feature, *Pungryu* can continue to be a genuine source of the spirit that guides Koreans to be natural, spontaneous, creative, harmonious and compassionate. Although they do not necessarily refer to this indigenous notion of *Pungryu* as a curative factor and health construct, some Korean expressive art therapists are working in this orientation by integrating traditional arts into their activities and always focusing on the notion of arts and play and inspire young future mental health professionals. The experience of *Pungryu*, in this case, mediated by Korean traditional artistic actions, combined with other methods such as meditation can be a fine alternative to existing conventional Western approaches. While *Pungryu* can be enjoyed individually, it is commonly best experienced in group through playing together as 'We (*Uri*)' whereby *Heung* (intrinsic sense of joy) underlined as the ingenious Korean psychology is easily raised. In this sense, *Pungryu*, *Heung* and *Uri*, on which Koreans place great importance, function as three indigenous curative elements. Experience of these three elements should be unique in its therapeutic potential, providing suffering minds with a way to reach the sense of solidarity, solace, and so liberation from suffering. The significance of *Pungryu* in contemporary Korean psychotherapy is especially related to the expression of naturalness and lightness, like a child at arts play. For Nietzsche, maturity is to reassume the seriousness one enjoyed as 'a child' at play, the childlike spirit that has natural joy and infinite creativity. Contemporary Koreans, however, incarnate only the image of 'collectors of burdens and lords in their own desert', that of 'the camel' and 'the lion' spiritual metamorphoses[6] described by Nietzsche.

Resuming the indigenous knowledge considered essential for the present history is to open possibilities to create something different from what is familiar and comfortable and ensure the authentic knowledge that teaches wisdom for use in modern existential struggles. What is therapeutic seems identical from one culture to another. And yet, ways and means of reaching it may differ. This is an attempt not just to understand the past but to find a tool for use, an indication of a curative path that resonates with Koreans within their cultures and circumstances. By 'Korean' psychotherapy, it does not imply a reactive struggle to defeat other forces or influences, but tries to refine a sustained act of approaching light and being affirmative to the Korean. Furthermore, to create psychotherapy service conditions that accommodate not only those who can afford but also those who do not have the means, it is vital to address inequality ingrained into the fabric of Korean society, and revive a critical mind for the current mental health system that has still little and limited concern towards those who are mentally ill and poor. They are clearly the more oppressed, marginalised *Ssial* in the present history of Korea. The whole of individuals, community and society should feel suitably chastened and realise that they are absolutely liable for paying attention to those *Ssials* and their suffering.

Notes

1 Michel Foucault invoked Bentham's 'Panopticon' as a metaphor for modern 'disciplinary' societies and their pervasive inclination to observe and normalise: 'On the whole, therefore, one can speak of the formation of a disciplinary society in this movement that stretches from the enclosed disciplines, a sort of social "quarantine", to an indefinitely generalisable mechanism of "panopticism".' Michel Foucault (1975): 'Surveiller et punir: Naissance de la Prison'.

2 According to the Mental disorder status survey conducted in 2011, almost one in three adults (27.6 per cent) in Korea suffered from some form of mental disorder at some point in their lives (31.7 per cent for men, 23.5 per cent for women) and only 15.3 per cent of people with psychiatric disorders would seek help from professionals (source from KOSIS (Korean Statistical Information Services)).

3 The same Mental disorder status survey in 2011 revealed that 15.6 per cent of adults have seriously thought about committing suicide more than once in their lives, 3.3 per cent of them have planned suicide and 3.2 per cent of them have actually attempted suicide. Over the past one year 3.7 per cent of the adults have seriously considered taking their own lives and 0.7 per cent of them have planned it while 0.3 per cent of them have attempted suicide. It is estimated that 108,000 adults have attempted suicide over the past one year. 57.0 per cent of those who have thought about suicide, 73.7 per cent of those who have planned suicide and 75.3 per cent of those who have attempted suicide have turned out to have experienced mental disorders. The suicide rates increased from an average of 13.1 per 100,000 in 1997 to 31.2 in 2010, and this trend was observed in all adult age groups.

The major cause for the impulse to commit suicide was illness and disability for those in the sixties; economic difficulties for the forties and the fifties; work-related issues for the twenties; school records and exams for the teens.

4 According to the report of 'The 2011 Epidemiological Survey of Mental Disorders in Korea' prepared by the Ministry of Health and Welfare, 15.3 per cent of the respondents (comprising a total 6,022 aged between 18 and 74: 2,308 of male and 3,714 of female) with mental disorders had been treated by psychotherapy or counselling at the time of interview. It has been raised by more than 6.0 per cent than the rate of that of 5 years ago. The rate of service use remains low in comparison with the rates in other countries, e.g., America 39.2 per cent (National Survey on Drug Use and Health 2010),

Australia 34.9 per cent, and New Zealand 38.9 per cent (WHO World Mental Heath Survey 2010–11).

5 Gilles Deleuze's *Différence et Répétition* (1968) introduces the importance of a philosophy of difference by describing how difference may be internal to the nature of each concept and how every idea may have multiple elements that may be differentiated. He goes on to define repetition as 'difference without a concept'. Repetition is thus reliant on difference more deeply than it is opposed. Deleuze explains that difference and repetition have a reality that is independent of the concepts of sameness, identity, resemblance, similarity, or equivalence. Pure difference is neither a factor of negativity nor a negation of sameness. Rather, it affirms the actuality of an idea. In Deleuzian way, difference is fundamentally viewed as the object of affirmation and not of negation.

6 Nietzsche introduced the three phases of spiritual metamorphose in his book *Thus Spoke Zarathustra* (1883–85): 54–55, symbolically represented by the camel, the lion and the child.

Bibliography

Deleuze, G. (1964, 1976). *Proust et les Signes* [Proust and the Signes]. Paris: Presses Universitaires de France.

Deleuze, G. (1968, 2000). *Différence et Répétition* [Difference and Repetition]. Paris: Presses Universitaires de France.

Foucault, M. (1975, 1993). *Surveiller et punir: Naissance de la Prison* [Discipline and Punish: The Birth of the Prison]. Paris: Gallimard.

Hoare, Q., & Nowell-Smith, G. (1971). *Selections from the prison notebooks of Antonio Gramsci.* New York: International Publishers.

Glossary

Chemyeon 체면 Social face inflicted from shame consciousness covering the natural emotional expressions.

Cheon-Ji-In 천지인 (天地人) Heaven–Earth–Human being as all connected in the Oneness.

Choung 충 (忠) Loyalty or devotion of the subordinate to superiors.

Gi 기 (氣) Matter or life force, energy, dynamic activity as the fundamental substance of the universe.

Haan 한 (恨) Deep emotional state of suppressed and accumulated anger, resentment or grief.

Haan-puri 한풀이 The process of releasing Haan, to unknot and let it out.

Han 한 (韓) One or whole, basic common thought system which underlies to become one, integrated, reconcile or harmonise with others.

Heung 흥 (興) Intrinsic sense of joy connoting humour and laughter.

Hwabyung 화병 Korean culture-bound psychiatric syndrome of 'anger disease'.

Hyo 효 (孝) Filial piety or devotion of the child to the parents.

Il-Shim 일심 (一心) 'One-Mind' of non-dualistic nature, philosophy by Wonhyo in the seventh century.

In 인 (仁) Highest ideal of Confucianism, virtue or benevolence, authoritative conduct or to act authoritatively.

Jeong 정 (情) Strong feeling of affection or attachment, special interpersonal bond of closeness.

Jung 정 (精) Body essence and sexual energy.

Kut 굿 Shamanic rite.

Mudang 무당 Shaman.

Noonchi 눈치 Intuitive perception to evaluate people's or social situations and to gauge the mood and states of mind through implicit cues.

Nori 놀이 Play.

Onmaeum 온마음 Whole mind.

Pungryu 풍류 (風流) Living naturally like the way the wind blows and the flow goes, a lifestyle in harmony and enjoyment with an emphasis on its meaning in art and nature.

Samul-nori 사물놀이 Percussion music play performed with four traditional Korean musical instruments – Buk, Janggu, Jing, and Kkwanggwari.
Seon 선 (禪) Zen, meditative state.
Seong 성 (性) Innate nature.
Ssial 씨알 Lit. seed, commoners or grassroots.
Suhn 선 (仙) Lit. 'person in/to mountain, spirit of freedom and peace while enjoying arts play amid pristine nature.
Tao 도 (道) Way, path or route, the primordial essence or fundamental nature of the universe.
Uri 우리 We-ness, sense of togetherness or oneness of Jeong-based relationship.
Wu-wei 무위 (無爲) Non-doing, non-action, non-interference or letting be.
Ye 예 (禮) Custom, propriety, morals or rules of proper behaviour.
Yi 이 (理) Underlying reason and principle, order of nature as reflected in its organic forms.

Index

FSC
www.fsc.org
MIX
Papier | Fördert gute Waldnutzung
FSC® C083411

Kolibri 360 GmbH
Ferdinand-Jühlke-Straße 7
99095 Erfurt, Deutschland
produktsicherheit@kolibri360.de